Raising Kids with Cochlear Implants:
Personal Narratives from a Family's Journey

Amy Milani, Ph.D.

DEDICATION

Dedicated to the parents of Generation CI.

CONTENTS

ACKNOWLEDGMENTS

This book is a gift to my children, Marcus and Lorna whose tremendous achievements can scarcely be conveyed with words.

I recognize the significant role of my husband, Hayes Milani in this project. His enduring belief in my artistic ability along with endless patience have finally been rewarded. As my companion in raising our children and in decisions regarding their cochlear implants, Hayes' remarkable courage has been vital to me.

I am grateful for the sound advice and encouragement of my manuscript readers. Each contributed considerably in our journey with hearing loss. Mary Ruth Leen inspired us to move to California and enroll in the preschool where she was teaching children with cochlear implants to listen and speak. Kathy Berger as head of school helped us manage our children's speech and language goals and advocate for their rights. Sharon Nutini, whose exceptional kindness and generosity as my daughter's first speech therapist gave us much strength. Jennifer Philpott, pediatric audiologist, readied my daughter for mainstreaming in her innovative classroom and auditory therapy sessions. Our current audiologist, Stacy Payne maximizes my children's hearing with a dedicated and passionate spirit.

Finally, I acknowledge my parents, Arnold and Shirley Peterson for teaching me how powerful parental love can be.

INTRODUCTION

Facing life as it comes is a true test of strength. The words are clear enough.

"Your child can't hear."

After thirteen years, the words are still hard to fathom. I remember how they sank deep into my heart. In an instant, life's kaleidoscope shifted-- permanently. My child can't hear. Simple, yet powerful words setting me spiraling down an unknown road to do battle with my son's bilateral profound hearing loss. Two years later, my daughter was born without hearing. I kept asking, "What can I do?" Decisions my husband and I made in those early months have changed the course of our children's lives.

I remember feeling overwhelmed by my desire for more information and I believe this type of experience is common. Parents may lack support exactly when they need it the most. I was lucky to eventually connect with a group of parents who provided an empathetic support system at a school for the deaf where children learn to listen and speak with their cochlear implants. As we moved through similar experiences together, the school's outstanding staff guided us in a productive direction. Most parents do not have an oral school for the deaf in their neighborhood. This book is a way for me to reach out to everyone who needs a hand in the unfamiliar world of cochlear implants.

I have witnessed both of my children transitioning from deaf to listening and speaking. I was present as the metamorphosis took place, not just as a passive spectator of their progress but an active participant. My husband and I decided our children would be implanted as soon as they were able. We carefully selected the professionals to guide our course of action. We moved from Germany, where our children were born and diagnosed with profound hearing loss, to California so they could attend an Oral Deaf school. Our choices made a significant difference in their development. We made those decisions without much assurance. Yet, they took courage and sacrifice from us.

Cochlear implants require total commitment from a child's parents or caretaker. At the time my son was diagnosed with profound hearing loss, I knew no one to ask about the difficulties of raising a child with a bionic ear. I never discussed the details of our daily routine with our doctors. Without personal experience, they could not advise us on the changes the implant would have on the quality of our lives. We entrusted them with our children's diagnosis, treatment, technical maintenance and speech therapy. Yet, when everything was going according to plan, we were alone with our uncertainties. Life with a high tech ear is not a straight and simple road. Parents need a glimpse of what is to come, both the joy and the adversity. My stories will empower them with such knowledge.

Experience has taught me that learning to listen and speak with a cochlear implant takes time. Each day brings new challenges. Although my journey is far from over, I have learned important lessons and gained valuable insight along the way. Stories I share in this book. I am proud my son and daughter are a part of "Generation CI", a generation of children implanted in infancy who are redefining expectations for those born with profound hearing loss. This book reveals how my children live with cochlear implant technology and how it impacts my family. Our story is proof of the remarkable strides being made towards eradicating hearing loss. Children like mine are the next chapter in the history of deafness.

Cochlear implants are without a doubt one of the most incredible life altering technologies but they also break, malfunction and fail the children who rely on them. No matter how well they adapt to listening with the device, my children cannot hear when they take off the body worn equipment. My husband and I have managed every situation outside the classroom, doctor's office, and therapy room on our own. We have never regretted our decision to be a fundamental part of our children's transition into hearing and speaking members of society. With newborn hearing screenings, parents have the opportunity to begin early intervention immediately. When they do so, the results can be remarkable. Preparing parents for their role as caretakers is a key component of success.

This book is an early intervention tool for families of recently diagnosed infants with hearing loss who are considering cochlear implant technology. Between the time our son's hearing loss was identified and his surgery took place at eleven months, my husband and I evaluated his options. We considered how different paths would affect the outcome of his life. Because my children are now eleven and thirteen years old, I write with a sense of perspective, reflecting on the impact of those early years. Themes in this book were inspired by journal entries and situations that continuously occurred over years of living with cochlear implant technology. Although illustrated by personal stories, I describe circumstances common to many children who have bionic ears. Parents, as you read this book, know I have walked in your shoes. Professionals in education and healthcare, get a glimpse of what your students and patients are actually experiencing.

The aim of this book is to make clear what the choice for a cochlear implant would mean, not just for a child but also for the family taking care of that child. Of the many factors determining the extent to which cochlear implant technology helps a child overcome hearing loss, such as early implantation, precise audiology, and intensive oral speech therapy, a dedicated home environment matters most. A one-year old child using cochlear implant equipment to hear needs supportive caretakers. Speech and language deficiencies are addressed step by step, requiring constant collaboration with doctors, teachers, and therapists. I practiced with my children at home and maintained their equipment until they were old enough to take over the responsibility. Although less intensively, I still devote time to audiology appointments, meetings with teachers and finding batteries to keep my children's equipment working.

In this book, I simulate the emotional ups and downs of my family's extraordinary journey by giving both sides of the story equal time. I begin with the diagnosis of my son's hearing loss, sharing the details of his progress as recorded in my journal from the year following his cochlear implant surgery. However, I cannot boast of his achievements without acknowledging the day-to-day struggles we experienced as a family. Alternating chapters contain lessons learned from the unavoidable challenges we encountered such as managing the cochlear implant equipment and the social implications for both children. Without acknowledging the difficulties, their success cannot be fully realized. I no longer take the smallest amount of progress for granted because I have witnessed how cochlear implants change lives. I know because my children's voices connect me to their hearts and minds. I hope through this book, they will speak to you.

1

Finding the Strength to Begin

Life altering events take the wind from your sails, leaving you emotionally exhausted. A new path is forced upon you and it hurts. Welcomed or not, a dramatic change in the course of your life requires a period of adjustment. When my son was diagnosed with hearing loss, I had to dig deep and find the strength to begin because every day that passed was time lost to silence. How you react to the news your child can't hear makes a tremendous difference on the outcome of their life. If you choose a cochlear implant for your child, you will need to awaken their sense of hearing through purposeful action. You must let go of feelings that may discourage you. Know it can be done. You will find tremendous satisfaction in making choices for your child and helping them succeed. Strength can be found in following your instincts, taking action of any sort, and knowing you and your child can endure the cochlear implant surgery.

    <u>Listen to your instincts.</u> Newborn hearing screenings are a good thing for children with hearing loss but they force parents to face their fears straightaway. The arrival of a baby is an intense time of adjustment for any family. Add a serious health concern to that experience and parents can find themselves in a very precarious position. Our first child was born in a small town set along the picturesque Rhein River in Germany. At that time, in the year 2000, our hospital offered a newborn hearing screening but it wasn't a required test. As I interacted with my beautiful baby in the hospital room, instincts led me to believe he wasn't responding to my voice. I watched for signs and alerted the doctor. I was told to not worry. My baby was handsome and strong with the perfect birth weight born the day after his due date. Of course he could hear. However, the obstetrician would do a quick examination before I went home. My son sat on my lap as the doctor clapped behind us. Sure enough, my little one moved in response. The physician dismissed my doubts without a second thought. I was left alone with my uncertainty. I wanted to believe everything was fine. Why listen to an instinct when professionals tell you--with a certain condescending tone, your baby can hear?

    When we arrived home, my head filled with questions. What if "the experts" somehow misdiagnosed my son's ability to hear? What if I was right? If he can hear, why doesn't he react to sound? I immediately began scanning through information about hearing loss online. The Internet turned out to be my greatest ally. I could research our options and discuss them with my husband without feeling led in one direction or another. I came across information on the cochlear implant but I dismissed the idea my child had a profound hearing loss. I knew of no one in our families who had serious issues with their hearing. After days of searching for answers, it was clear we should go ahead and request an Oto Acoustic Emissions

(OAE) test or newborn hearing screening from a local Ears Nose Throat specialist (ENT). It was an inexpensive assessment and would not be uncomfortable for our child. Most importantly, it would tell us objectively if he could hear. I was sure the test results would put my doubts finally to rest.

In the weeks leading up to our appointment, my misgivings lingered. I observed my son more carefully. I tried to wake him with loud sounds- dropping a book or rattling a toy. I looked for reactions to my voice. All day I searched for signs he could hear. Within a month, we had an appointment with the neighborhood ENT and were ready to have a definitive test run. As I held my sleeping son, the doctor inserted small ear buds or "insert earphones" into his ears while we anxiously watched the computer screen. The program produced sounds but his cochlea or inner ears did not respond with an echo, as they should have. Our son failed the screening, signifying there was indeed an issue with his hearing. My husband and I knew my instincts had been right from the start. To our surprise, the ENT insisted the test results were a false negative. He believed our child was too young with ears so small and undeveloped at one month that the test could be rendered inconclusive. Fluid in the ears can also interfere with the test results. He recommended we return in another month and retake the test. After my son failed the second screening, our ENT finally gave us the name of a specialist who would perform a different test to tell us exactly what he could hear.

Listening to my instincts led us to do the right thing and have our child's hearing tested. Instincts help us protect our loved ones and ourselves. There are many outside influences instructing us how to best raise our children, such as books on parenting, daytime TV, respected pediatricians, social playgroups, and the Internet. We can lose faith in our ability to judge a situation and know what type of help is warranted. Since there is no one right way to raise a child, doubts can overwhelm. When I learn about a child who was not diagnosed until age five with profound hearing loss, I wonder how often a parent had instinctual feelings their young one could not hear but had them dismissed by another well-meaning but ineffectual advisor, physician, friend, or family member.

Parents, you know your child best. If there are signs of hearing loss, get answers and get help. There are simple painless tests that will tell you objectively, without a doubt if your child can hear-- even in infancy. Don't hesitate having your child retested to be sure of the findings. Seek out professionals who respect your beliefs and are willing to work alongside you, not treat your concerns as obtuse or bothersome. These people will be members of your child's "team". They will provide support and help you find the courage to move forward. Your instincts rarely fail you.

Take action. It was clear, I couldn't waste any more time waiting and watching for signs my son could hear. All my sources agreed-- the more quickly a child is diagnosed and treated for hearing loss, the more successful the results. I went ahead and scheduled the second hearing test, called an Auditory Brainstem Response (ABR) test. I wasn't nervous as my child was given just enough medication to lull him to sleep before the screening. In order to help him, I would need to know exactly what was happening inside his tiny ears and this test would give us those answers. When he was fully relaxed, a range of sounds were sent again via ear buds or insert earphones into the ear canals to measure how well they would travel along the hearing nerve to the brain. Small sensors gently taped to his head could read this information through the skin. Each pitch was tested from soft to loud. The results of the ABR gave us startling news-- my child had total hearing loss in both ears. Clinicians refer to his condition as bilateral sensorineural hearing loss, meaning he was born with inner ears that aren't able to transport sounds to the brain. The tiny hairs that tickle the nerve sending information up the hearing pathway were simply broken or not there. However, the test showed my son's hearing nerve was healthy and this fact would later become a critical qualifier for the cochlear implant.

Taking action was easy once we were on track in the German healthcare system. Germans don't consider hearing an "optional" choice for deaf babies. Priority is given to medically help a child hear through whatever technology available. German culture is inherently hierarchical and doctors are viewed with unquestionable respect as experts. It was my impression that once a physician recommends a cochlear implant, German families do not consider other options. At the time, all children born deaf were potential candidates for cochlear implants unless they physically could not be implanted. Surgery was covered by universal health care eliminating financial barriers.

German healthcare policy echoed our own sentiments and we felt comfortable with the advise of our doctors. We were fortunate to be in a country with surgeons quite experienced with implanting infants. Although cochlear implants have been a successful treatment for profound hearing loss in the United States as well, American families have more choices and options. I have experienced a broad spectrum of approaches to hearing loss in American federal and private programs with less standardization across the country than in Germany. Most importantly, American public school classrooms, unlike those in Germany are required by law to include all types of children. As a global issue, families of deaf infants around the world must take action within a given healthcare system and cultural context.

Regardless of where you may be living, a couple facing a serious health issue in their child requires great tenacity. No one imagines his or her baby being born with a serious health concern. It shakes the foundation of a family. A newborn symbolizes a fresh start in life and the unlimited possibilities of the future. It is much easier and certainly more convenient to push aside unwanted doubts about your child's health. With hearing loss, quick action will pay off. Do what it takes to help your child. Make those appointments with an audiologist and keep them. Above all, find strength in your spouse if you can- know that with a partner you are more effective and persuasive. You may have to argue with doctors, push for immediate screenings or audiology appointments and challenge results that don't match what you have observed in your child. Resist searching for blame in the family tree or creating an emotional distance to protect you. From now on, you will be working together for and with your child to manage the diagnosis of hearing loss. Finding strength in each other will be critical down the road when patience is worn thin. If you are coping with your baby's hearing loss as a single parent, consider who you can rely upon when extra support and encouragement is needed. Believe in your instincts and take action.

Surviving surgery. On a visit back to the United States shortly after my son's diagnosis, I met with a highly recommended audiologist. Her final words stayed with me, "Find a doctor in Germany who is willing to schedule your son's cochlear implant surgery as soon as possible. Earlier is better!" I took this advice to heart. My child was eleven months at the time of his surgery. In 2001, German doctors were already well versed in cochlear implantation and had been performing surgeries on infants for years. In the U.S., the FDA guidelines recommended the age of 18 months for a cochlear implant.

At the time, we had no idea how fortunate we were to be living in Germany, giving our child the gift of hearing six months earlier than if we had been in the States. What seemed like an insignificant difference in the scope of a life actually had a tremendous impact on my son's eventual audition skills and speech production. In most cases, the younger a child is implanted, the quicker the brain learns to comprehend and produce language. For this reason, infants as young as six months old undergo cochlear implant surgery. Consider all an infant can learn in one day, especially about language and sounds in the environment. Time squandered can be detrimental for a child with hearing loss.

The months before my son's surgery passed slowly. He was immediately fitted with hearing aids for a six months trial period, although they were much trouble for little benefit. Even the most powerful hearing aids could not help him hear high-pitched or soft speech sounds like /s/, /f/, and /th/. I remember struggling to keep the enormous hearing aids on his tiny ears and coping with the trill of "feedback" squealing from ear molds that never fit properly. I knew he wasn't hearing much through the hearing aids, so I communicated more by touch and facial expressions. I interacted with him constantly and always had him near me so he could watch what I was doing. I was determined to keep involved with all sorts of baby activities. He participated in playgroups and traveled with us to Italy, Scotland and France.

We finally met with our surgeon, Dr. Jan Kiefer at the hospital in Frankfurt. He was kind and patient even when I bombarded him with lots of questions. My son's hearing loss was the same in both ears. He would only have one side implanted, as was standard. Dr. Kiefer recommended implanting the right cochlea. As I marked the surgery date on our calendar, I felt my heart quicken. I knew my son would be ready to hear but would I be equipped to help him through it all?

Finally, the surgery was upon us. We drove to the hospital in Frankfurt through the early morning fog. I had to believe we were doing the right thing for our family but it felt like leaping off a cliff. Ten months had past since my son's diagnosis. Ten months of waiting behind me. Even so, entrusting a surgeon with your 11 month-old is a hard thing to do. When I looked back at my tiny son securely sleeping in his car seat, somehow it seemed too soon and too radical to undergo such a serious treatment. Even when your heart tells you it's the right decision. Don't put off the date because the thought of your baby in surgery stops you cold. Realize it will never be easy.

I know from personal experience, one of the most difficult barriers for parents to overcome in the process of moving forward with a cochlear implant is the surgery. Once your child is destined for a cochlear implant, there is plenty to do. Gather all types of information by reading books, searching online, visiting auditory oral programs, meeting with auditory verbal therapists, talking to parents, and attending conferences. Prepare yourself as best you can for what's ahead. Don't get distracted by the thought of surgery. At a coffeehouse in the hospital, my husband and I waited to hear news from the doctors during the longest four hours of my life! The discussions about our options were done for now. When the surgery was over, there would be no going back. Our child would have a cochlear implant connected to his inner ear for the remainder of his life.

After the surgery, our doctors reassured us the implant had been tested and was working perfectly. When they carefully handed my child back to me, he was still groggy. The enormous bandage on his head made him look like a war veteran, not a new member of the hearing world. Did he feel pain, I wondered? For a week, he and I stayed together in the hospital. He would not be able to hear until the audiologist activated the implant and programmed the speech processor. I often held my son to me tightly, hoping he could feel how much I loved him. The German hospital was clean and practical, not particularly accommodating for mother and baby. Even so, our extended stay gave him the opportunity to heal while we remaining insulated from the world.

The surgery represents a serious commitment to spoken language as it alters the inner structure of your child's cochlea. The surgery leaves a scar as evidence of the damage within, although less significant now with new surgical techniques. My son's baby fine hair barely covered his head at the time of his surgery. It was not easy to see the wound healing behind his ear and know he had experienced some discomfort. Yet, we realized in the end, time was on our side.

Gradually, I understood that both child and parents require healing after the surgery. Physical wounds eventually mend and the infant has little to no recollection of their hospital ordeal. More lasting is the emotional wound a parent has from worry and apprehension over the unknown, even when the child's treatment for hearing loss is moving forward according to plan. Later that month, our audiologist assured us our child's cochlear implant was activated and he could hear. I thought about how the real labor would soon begin. No more waiting, it was time to get to work.

Key Points to Consider

1. Listen to your instincts if you believe your child has hearing loss and request an **OAE** test.

2. Find like-minded healthcare professionals and begin early intervention as soon as possible.

3. Don't delay in scheduling your child's cochlear implant surgery.

2

My First Year Journal: Our Favorite Things

One year and four months old.

Four months with the implant.

After four months with the implant, I am sure my child understands pieces of my speech. There are specific words that now have meaning for him. These words represent some of his favorite activities we do together, activities we regularly enjoy as part of our routine that have somehow made a big impression on his little mind. There is a joy in recognition, in understanding and in performing a task that has meaning. He uncovers important elements in the world and gives them a name- a word he hears me say over and over. Our lives have repetition and this regularity helps him learn. In the same way, there are sounds that are not proper words but have

9

meaning in our play, during our reading, in videos and heard in our environment. He attempts to reproduce a sound to imitate a distinctive noise in the home and outdoors, such as the roar of an airplane. These sounds are words to him and they carry just as much meaning, representing specific objects. Similarly, the sounds animals make to communicate are, in a funny way, rudimentary words to him, more easily produced and again remembered through repetition. Of all the daily experiences my child encounters, he is beginning to discern those that have value for him, such as the impressiveness of a jet flying overhead or a semi rumbling down the highway. All of these "words" represents his favorite things for this moment in time.

Yet, progress is slower than I would like. His motivation to learn about the world seems to drive his acquisition of language, following the instincts of natural exploration. I know he cannot spend all his time learning to listen. Just eighteen months old, he is equally fascinated with how his body moves and the flood of new sensations he experiences every day. I notice his interest in language peaks only when all other modes of communication are exhausted, such as crying and gesturing. I reluctantly prepare myself for times when he has no interest in listening. l know he will acquire language in spurts. He will be satisfied for a time with what he understands and then suddenly, his awareness of the world will broaden and he will listen more carefully to the sounds of my speech. I have designated a journal to track his development. My journal reminds me that he is indeed making progress.

The first list in my journal contains real words representing the activities that most engage my child's attention: tree, book, water, clock, shoe, ball, and hot. These words have great meaning to him and I notice how he responds to them over and over. Although my child has heard them for the first time through his cochlear implant, they are no different from the first words most children learn. Unlike mothers who can rely on natural exposure to these words, I leave nothing to chance. I purposefully provide him with the opportunity to experience the words during our daily routine. When I show him something new, I have him feel it and understand it as I tell him what it is. I know his tactile memory will help him learn the word for it. I believe in the power of repetition and I integrate specific activities into our daily practice of his favorite words.

Tree

One of his favorite things to do is play in a park at the edge of a forest near our home in Germany. The woods are a place of great discovery. My child loves the sensations he experiences outside. He feels the bark of a tree or splashes his hand in a puddle. Squirrels and dogs entertain him with their behavior. Each time he engages with something outside, I feed in a "trigger" word to represent the experience. It's no surprise the word "tree" symbolizes the great outdoors- where all the senses are highly stimulated. At the park, my son digs, swings, and feels the grass. I see his head turned upward and notice how he seeks the source of a sound new to him. I watch how he listens to a bird perched high above us. I feel thrilled following his eyes move at the sound of wind in the trees. The cochlear implant has made these sensations possible and has given him a deeper connection to nature. During this time, I understand the power of his implant. I realize how I can help him. When we are outside, I find ways to incorporate the word "tree" into our play: "Look at the squirrel up in the tree!", "Let's run to the big tree!", or "The leaves are falling from the tree." Saying "tree" over and over in different sentences helps my child learn its meaning in context, in natural circumstances, through normal dialogue.

Book

Books are a real source of language. My son understands books are for learning. We read together daily. He learns how to pick out a book, hold it steady and turn pages, returning it to the shelf after we are through. This routine is symbolized by the word "book". My child often brings a book over to read spontaneously. I feed in, "Do you want mommy to read you this book? I love to read this book. This is my favorite book. It's such a big book. Look at the elephant on the cover of this

11

book. Can you open the book?" It is easy for him to hear the word, "book" at the end of each sentence. He can recognize the blend of sounds separately from the rest and the pitch in my voice accentuates it. Books also allow us to practice his other favorite words, such as "tree".

Water

"Water" is big part of life. My child drinks it, bathes in it, splashes it, and sees it fall from clouds in the sky. He watches me use water for cooking and cleaning. He tastes it and feels it. He senses the temperature of water as steam rises from a pot or drips from the faucet. For each water-based activity, I feed him the word "water" in my speech. "Are you thirsty, do you want water? How about a cup of water? There you go, drink some water. How cold is the water?" I know my child feels powerful understanding the word, "water". Even in his innocence, he recognizes our need for water.

Clock

Sitting at my feet in the kitchen, my child notices the changing numbers of the digital clock on our stove. I point to the digits and tell him, "Do you see the number 5 on the clock?" These numbers introduce time: dinner time, nap time, and time for the cookies to come out of the oven. He looks at the numbers on my watch and I tell him, "That's mama's clock" knowing he can learn the word "watch" later. I want him to see patterns in the world and understand that he will notice more than one place where numbers mean time. When I sense he is ready to learn more, I will tell him how my watch lets me know what time it is.

Shoe

The word representing a trip outside for my child is "shoe". By this time, he is familiar with our household routine and putting shoes on means leaving the house. Trying to exert control over his life, he quickly learns what it takes to escape the confinement indoors. I distinctly remember testing his receptive recognition of words by asking him to do a task. I said without gestures and without facing him, "Put your shoes on so we can go outside." He immediately got up and walked over to his shoes. What a thrill!

Ball

One game we play inside and out is catch. My child loves to throw a ball, so he needs to know the word to understand the activity we will be playing. We have balls of every shape and size. There is no end to the entertainment we create with balls. He can kick, throw, roll, hide, bounce, and chase them. He even tries to steal them from other children at the park. There can never be enough balls in our house. Playing with a ball is the perfect way to model dialogue. First I have the ball, then he has the ball, then I have it and so on. As we pass the ball back and forth, my son learns how to dialogue. First I say something, then he says something, and then I say something in return. The movement echoes the natural flow of communication between us. Each time the ball comes to me, I use the word "ball": "Toss mommy the ball. What a big ball! Catch the ball." Even when I know he can't say the words yet, I pause when it's his turn. I wait for the day when he will respond with, "Mama, play ball!"

At this point, I continuously watch for signs of understanding or his "receptive" comprehension. It can often be difficult to tell if he grasps what I am saying. His eyes light up, he may vocalize, or gesture with his hand to let me know he's following my words. He loves to point and I can tell he believes pointing is the way to get what he wants. I try not reacting to his point, instead encouraging the use of words. I will ask him, "What do you want? Hmmm, I don't understand." Even when I know perfectly well he wants another cookie. I talk to him incessantly, especially about his favorite things. I look for reactions...physical, verbal, and emotional. I try to repeat the words I think he understands to trigger a response in him. I speak to him so he can't see my face and I keep track in my journal. I remind myself each new word he comprehends is a true accomplishment. Sometimes, I don't feel patient enough. I want to know what he is thinking, what's going on *inside that bright mind of his. I want him to tell me.*

My child is also trying to say his favorite words. Usually, he is able to say a simple vowel and consonant combination, which most likely are the sounds in the word he can most easily hear. I try to fill in the rest by modeling the correct pronunciation of the word, so he can hear all the sounds. Every time he tries to say something I react. I want to encourage this behavior. I want to show him that he can get my attention by speaking. I want to reward his speech with affirmation. Although it's not always easy, I make it a priority to encourage his attempts at speech. After so many months of hearing nothing, I want him to begin participating in the human privilege we call dialogue.

Hot

My child loves to play at my feet while I cook, so naturally our kitchen is where he learned the meaning of the word "hot". His eyes widen when I bring steaming food to the table, as the radiating heat reaches his skin. "Hot" is one of the first words my child attempts to say. He verbalizes "ot" or "ah" when he sees things on the stovetop or in the oven. I celebrate his expressive use of language by feeding in sentences so he can hear the pronunciation of the word: "The chicken soup is hot! Be careful, it may be hot! Wow, you're right, that's hot!" In this way, I am affirming his use of the word for this particular situation. I can see that he enjoys expressing the concept of hot.

Up

My child also verbalizes the word "up" when he wants to go up or down. He says it when he wants to go up or down stairs, when he is interested in crawling up on the couch or up onto my lap. He also will say "up" to get out of his high chair. I suppose children of his age often feel physically stuck and the lack of coordination prevents them from getting to where they want to go. Even with fierce independence and determination, a child will recognize they need help especially after one or two failed attempts. Frustration actually motivates a child to learn. Use this time to teach your child a new word. It is the perfect opportunity to model the language needed in a particular situation: "Do you want to come up? Do you want to go up? Reach up. Get up." Look for the chance to teach your child a word when they are aggravated by the inability to do something by themselves. Withhold your help for a moment until you've completely captured your child's attention. Repeat the word you want them to say and affirm any attempts to say it with your eyes, your smile and your hands. Let your child know you are proud of them.

Onomatopoeia - a vocal imitation of a sound

My child strings vowels and consonants together to describe a sound he's heard using "onomatopoeia". He experiments with creating sound effects for sudden noises. Balloons are an endless source of play at our house. He laughs and laughs when my husband pops them. The sound must be startling heard clearly through his cochlear implant. He responds by saying, "pop". Outside, we blow bubbles and watch them float into the sky. When they reach a tree branch or the wall, he says, "pop" in anticipation. He also tries to say, "boom" when a toy hits the wood floor in our living room. Loud sounds in the environment get his attention and he wants me to know that he has heard them. A frequent backseat passenger in trips around town, my child consistently makes a noise for a car, "brrmm brrmm". He looks for planes flying overhead and tries to imitate the sound they make. He has become acutely aware that the world is full of noises. He has learned that all sounds have meaning and he pays close attention to what he hears.

Animal Sounds

Recently, my child shows an interest in learning about animals and the sounds they make. When I read a story and the snake character hisses, he tries to imitate my voice by saying, "s-s-s-s-s". This has been a great way to check if he is hearing soft high frequency sounds. Sitting together with a book, I ask him, "What animal says, 's-s-s-s-s-s'?" He points with certainty at a long green snake in the picture. When he doesn't understand what I say, my voice must sound to him like adults in the Peanuts cartoon, "wawa wawa wawa". It's amazing how well he has learned to listen and understand my speech. He does not have to look at my face to watch my lips forming the letters. He lets his cochlear implant do the work and more importantly he trusts what he is hearing.

My child has many opportunities to learn specific animal onomatopoeias in nursery rhymes like "Bah, Bah, Black Sheep" and with classic toys like The Farmer Says See 'N Say. Our German therapist brings many toy animals to work with him one on one. Although fluent in English, I wonder if she is the right person for us. Pulling out a small wooden rooster, she began teaching him to say "kikeriki" instead of "cockadoodledoo". If she doesn't even know what sounds Americans associate with animals, then how can she decipher the words he is trying to say? How can she understand American baby talk? I begin to wonder. Is it important? Does it really matter? Again, we choose the path of least resistance. She would be perfect if we wanted him to learn German. But for now, we would prefer an American speech therapist without an accent. I try to find one at the American military base and in the English language newspaper without any luck. He will have to learn English for now from our expatriate friends, his father and myself.

I notice my child continues to speak even when he can't hear. He doesn't seem to discriminate between having the device on or off when it comes to communicating. One evening in the bath, he was having so much fun playing with a rubber duck that he kept after me to make a duck noise, even "quacking" himself. He is less interested in speaking when he can't hear, but if he wants something from me he will continue to use his voice. I have to accept that my child's world is different than mine. I want him to feel comfortable when he's hearing as well as when he's not because that's his reality. It's me that has to adjust and find ways to communicate in every situation. However, I am diligent about putting the external pieces of his CI on first thing in the morning, checking to be sure it's working during the day and removing them just before he goes to bed at night. I want more than anything for *him to feel connected to others through sound.*

My child's "favorite words" hold a special place in my memory. The doubts and worries over our decision to have him use a cochlear implant subside as he begins to listen and speak. If his implant is working, I know he can learn in a natural way, as hearing children do. However, his speech is still behind his peers so we provide English language immersion at home. I know the world outside our garden gate is largely unaware of the cochlear implant. I experience its naivety and insensitivity first hand as my child's spokeswoman and advocate. In terms of our choices, we remain steadfast. Feeling sure of our mission and understanding the task at hand, we constantly work together to build upon his list of favorite words.

3

Becoming a Child's Advocate

Preoccupied with such an intense transition, how could I
have anticipated the way people would react to my son's
condition? Did I know how to advocate for him? I was not
prepared for all the commotion his hearing aids and cochlear
implant equipment would create. Busy finding my bearings, I
waded through new information and cared for my infant. It was
a time to turn inward and refocus priorities, create new goals
while making the best of each day. But the world was curious
and constantly invaded my personal space with a stream of
questions, comments and criticism. The days when I lacked my
usual drive to figure things out, I became acutely aware of the
outside pressures threatening to consume me. For the most
part, I felt energized by my ability to create a productive routine
for my family and by my love for my baby. Like any new

mother, I was learning each day what to do and how to handle different situations, ignoring the busy world in motion around me.

However, I frequently found myself confronted by people who offered insensitive comments about my child's hearing equipment or bombarded me with questions too personal in nature. Friends and family did not hide their shock at our situation begging for explanations and demanding details. Strangers on the streets of Wiesbaden were neither considerate nor compassionate. My daily experiences were tainted by the swift judgments and stark frankness of Germanic culture. I was angered and incensed by the boldness I often encountered. Not good with quick comebacks, I often stammered out elaborate answers, giving more intimate details than I wanted.

Later, I thought about how I could have responded better. I knew I would have to be prepared for future interrogations, as they would surely continue. After thirteen years, I still have to answer questions regarding my children's hearing loss and their cochlear implants. Although the inquiries bother me less, I still find myself amazed that curiosity supersedes sensitivity. I have also become more aware, when I spot a child who struggles with visually apparent health issues, of the parents who care for that child and how they might be experiencing life. More than a harsh inquiry, they might need a quick smile or compliment on their child's beauty in whatever form it takes. I have found that people are typically curious about the following three issues: the noticeable hearing aids or cochlear implant equipment my children must wear, the cause of hearing loss in our family and the challenges of raising children with hearing loss.

Physical differences. During the six-month period before his cochlear implant surgery, strangers regularly stopped me on the street to ask why my son was wearing hearing aids. I realized people are not comfortable seeing a child just over one year, peach fuzz still covering his head with huge hearing aids. To test my theory, I bought a small cap with ties for under the chin. As I wandered through the pedestrian streets of Wiesbaden on my daily shopping excursions, strangers told me what a beautiful child I had, his round face tightly encircled by his cap. I relished any fawning over my offspring, as any proud mother would. But on days when the cap was off, his handsome features were overlooked. People wanted to know why my child had hearing aids and how I had found out my baby couldn't hear. Most didn't seem to realize the importance of identifying hearing loss as soon as possible. A young child wearing hearing aids proves early intervention is well underway. In all my experiences early on, I never once met someone who acknowledged my child's hearing aids were sign of proactive parenting and a baby well cared for.

The cochlear implant equipment enabling my children to speak so naturally is the very thing setting them apart from other children their age. All three brands we considered have visible components. Since their first birthdays, my children have used a body worn "speech processor", as big as a deck of cards containing a computer chip run by batteries. Although the proportion of equipment to body size has decreased dramatically over the years, accommodations must still be made to wear it through all of life's circumstances. A wire runs from the processor up to a circular microphone the size of a thick quarter. Sound enters the microphone and eventually finds its way to the implant and hearing nerve. The plastic and metallic pieces confuse people and contradict what they know about hearing loss. After seeing the equipment and learning my children were born with a profound loss, they expect to hear a deficit in speech or articulation. To their surprise, my children's voices are clear and natural sounding. Until the cochlear implant is so widespread in its use that society understands what it means on sight, caretakers will have to explain how physical differences, namely outwardly visible equipment help a child to hear and speak.

The cochlear implant's microphone "magically" sits on the side of my son's head. Unlike the recognizable shape of hearing aids, his microphone is circular and rests directly over the place where the inner ear is located. It can definitely attract attention, depending on the hair length and style. When people notice the microphone, they are mystified by it. Unable to overlook something physically unusual, curiosity prompts them to inquire what it is. Someone once asked me if my son's microphone was a GPS for tracking him down. People usually don't think it's a sign of a serious health condition. Today, we are used to seeing small pieces of equipment in and around people's ears like the Bluetooth phone or ear buds for an iphone. Still, an infant with mechanical accessories draws interest. Meeting a person with a true desire to learn more about my child's bionic ear is unfortunately seldom encountered.

When someone asks, "What is that?" gesturing at my son's microphone, I know an answer is expected. Yet, there are many ways I can respond. If I feel irritated by the abrupt intrusion, I might say, "It's a solar power receptor to run his mechanical heart" or some other ridiculous quip. I cannot fathom the insensitivity of pointing at a young child and calling attention to something unusual on his or her body. Someone once asked me, "Is that thing attached to his head?" When I see their face ponder the possibilities, I think, "If it was, why would I be interested in talking about it with you?" If I am startled by a question, I must make a split second decision how to react. Another time, I was asked, "Is the implant in his brain?" Should my response be good natured or quick tempered, sarcastic or angered? A simple response might be, "It's for my child's hearing" or "It helps his hearing loss". As a naturally private person, I don't understand these confrontations but I have learned to expect them. For the most part, I keep my answers quick and direct, moving on before a deeper conversation evolves. Yet, I sometimes feel the need to explain the miracle my child is experiencing to those who are willing to listen. No matter how ignorant and insensitive people are, I hope they learn something about hearing loss from our conversation. It would certainly help my child and those like him if the world were more knowledgeable about cochlear implants.

Causes of hearing loss. Another line of questioning from friends and strangers is the cause of my children's hearing loss. People want to know why they can't hear. Early on, I learned the basics of sensorineural deafness, but I did not dwell on finding the reason why this situation "happened to me". I won't waste time trying to pinpoint the events that led to my life change. I just acknowledge them and move on. Even so, the world wonders why. Shortly after he was diagnosed with hearing loss, I was strongly encouraged by my doctor to spend the weekend with my son at an ENT clinic for research in Mainz, Germany. There he would undergo a battery of assessments, including genetic testing. When the doctors began their examinations, my normally content baby became extremely anxious and upset. I suddenly knew I didn't want him to experience pain and stress he wouldn't comprehend, especially while he could not hear. I discussed the situation with my husband and we left before the testing was completed. We had chosen a course of treatment for our child's hearing loss. No amount of assessments could change that now. Certainly, there is the need for further study of sensorineural hearing loss but my children can participate in research as adults if they wish to. I remain committed to the things that will actually help them now and will shelter them from harm as much as any mother would.

<u>Advocate for your child.</u> Most inquires into the cause of my children's hearing loss are not intended to be hurtful. I cannot expect people to know how I feel when they have not experienced my life. They will never understand how superficial such questions are to a mother trying to find her way. Still, my internal emotional barometer inevitably rises from their thoughtlessness. Forcing me to talk about something I am not comfortable explaining, I often feel personally bruised by such encounters.

For instance, people wonder how my children could be born deaf when my husband and I are not, asking, "Does deafness run in your family?" or "Is their hearing loss a genetic problem?" Again, I am startled by the bluntness. Questions of this type are one sided and make me feel defensive. My children's genetic makeup is partly my own and my family line is hardly something I want questioned. I cannot in turn respond by asking about their genetic idiosyncrasies so I am compelled to find an answer that curbs their curiosity. "Yes, genetics is the cause of their hearing loss." Simple and direct, my answer does not invite further discussion.

I know my children's genes are not only the reason for their hearing loss. They also make them bright and beautiful people.

Their genetic map has given them a starting point in life but will not determine what they make of it. We are all just unique blends of genetic heritage with traits that can be seen, as in the case of red hair and those that cannot, like the threat of breast cancer. Recessive genes produce children with rare traits of all kinds, making this world a more interesting and sometimes more challenging place.

My children are living billboards for cochlear implant technology. Because people can see their equipment, I have to be prepared to answer questions about it. I must be ready. No matter what, I cannot let outside attitudes shape who I am. I have made choices as a parent and I can live with those decisions. I am proud of my children and all they have accomplished with their cochlear implants. I am prepared to share their story and be their advocate. Over time, I have learned how to gauge how much information to reveal when the questions come and how to keep my privacy intact when needed. I can't worry about how people will react to what I say. If I don't feel up to the task, I remember my husband's wise advice, "It's okay not to answer everybody's questions!" Friends that truly care will wait for you to initiate a conversation about your child's hearing loss.

Key Points to Consider

1. Be prepared for questions about your child's noticeable hearing equipment.

2. Define your comfort zone before explaining the cause of your child's of hearing loss.

3. Learn how and when to advocate for cochlear implants.

4

My First Year Journal: Using Precise Words

One year and five months old.

Five months with the implant.

Confident my child comprehends a minimal amount of basic vocabulary, I make a conscious effort to teach him more precise words for the things he's most interested in. I can see he enjoys identifying objects accurately. If he already understands that "truck" represents all big vehicles with four wheels, then he's ready to learn specific types of trucks and visually recognize their differences. Although it's still enough to call a truck a truck, better yet to be identified by its function. When we take a walk along the busy streets of Wiesbaden, I point out how dump trucks, garbage trucks, or tow trucks are used for different purposes. I see his eyes widen as he studies their shapes, colors and sounds. It's my job to teach him the differences, point out what I notice about their features or emphasize important distinctions. For now, he looks to me as the expert and takes his role as the devoted student very seriously.

Why is it so important to express our thoughts precisely? Shakespeare argues, "What's in a name? That which we call a rose, by any other name would smell as sweet". No matter what name we give an object; it remains the same in form and substance. There is, however, cultural significance in selecting specific words to express a thought. My child notices brightly colored scented bits of beauty growing in the garden and learns these plants are called flowers. If he calls a rose "a flower" he is correct. Yet, a rose is a distinct flower with its own form and scent, having special significance and meaning attached to it. I pick one and hand it to him, so he knows a gift of roses is an expression of love. When my child is ready, I can tell him how a "Knock Out" rose would be a great addition to our flowerbed because of its tenacity and beauty. Talking about the same subject, my words progress from flower to rose to Knock Out Rose. I build his vocabulary naturally from general to specific. He will learn how specific he needs to be when he speaks.

There is something satisfying about finding the likeness in things, an order in the world amid all the chaos. My child looks for patterns everywhere like a game he plays that never loses its appeal. It's not always easy. Separating veggies on the table, I'm stumped. In what category does a red globe containing seeds or the tomato, belong-- vegetable or fruit? My child acts confidently in his knowledge of categories. He knows "books" go on the shelf with all the other volumes in our library. "Shells" of different sea creatures big and small go together in the bowl by the mirror and "sox" are stored together in the top drawer, whether striped or solid.

From a practical standpoint, grouping like things in the home make them easier to find. In the evening, I give my child items to clean up after a long day of experimentation and play. "Where does this go?" I ask, handing him an object. After appraising its weight and considering color and shape, he marches over to the box where his beloved building blocks are stored. Next time, he will know where to find it when his castle would look better with an extra high tower or thick fortification. In the small world that is our home, he has a good understanding of the categories that make his life easier.

My child naturally sorts the objects in his life. During our playtime, he establishes his categories by gathering like things together in a group. On his own, he pulls out all the toy cars from the bin, carefully lining them up along the edge of the area rug. The trucks and planes from the collection are left behind, not fitting his criteria for a small motor vehicle. I call out to him, "Are the cars going fast?" or "Do the cars go Beep Beep?" He answers with a "Brrrm, brrrm" and I know that's his word for car. I respond with, "What a pretty red car!"

It's no different at dinnertime when facing a plate full of vegetables. He pushes his peas to one side and carrots to the other with careful precision. Color and shape might be a strong indicator of food type, as he doesn't eagerly dive in for a taste. I can say, "eat your food" or "finish your vegetables" but he needs to let me know with specific words if he wants "more carrots." He is learning that "more food" might not produce the results he wants as I pile another helping of peas on his plate.

Right now, his favorite words are large categories containing many different items and these general words are exactly what he needs. By distinguishing how things around him are similar or different, my child creates categories in his mind to organize his thoughts. He must be overwhelmed by all the variety. Referring to things in broad categories helps him to make sense of all the variation. We naturally use a shared understanding of categories to communicate with each other.

Living abroad, I find myself forced to learn more specific words to get exactly what I need when shopping in local markets. To buy my family fresh bread, I walk down to our neighborhood Baeckerei or German bakery. Upon entering the shop, I am overwhelmed by all the colors, textures and scents that fall into the category of "bread". I have been told there are 2256 officially recognized types. As the morning crowd nudges me towards the counter, I realize I will have to learn the names of different breads to get the type I need: Roggenmischbrote, Volkornbrote, Weizenmischbrote,

Mehrkornbrote, Dinkelbrote, and Haferbrote, etc... My child nibbles on a soft pretzel while I place my order by pointing, reduced to the antics of a two year old. I have empathy for my child, as he must be frustrated not knowing specific words. He works for now on learning broad categories, such as "truck" to refer to all big rumbling vehicles just to keep things simple.

I name things with more specific vocabulary when I sense my child recognizes difference and wants to name it. I can usually see the frustration in his face. He looks at me with eyes pleading as he physically gestures towards the object of his desire. Sometimes, I play innocent although I know what he wants, using the word he understands, "Do you want a snack? "Hmm, what would be a good snack?" Then I expose him to a few new words. "How about a banana?" I say grabbing one from the kitchen counter. He looks at the slim yellow fruit with distain. "How about some cheese?" I say showing him choices from the refrigerator. No response. "Cookies? Is that what you want for a snack?" Jackpot! His head bobs and his eyes light up. I knew what he wanted. Besides exposing him to healthier options, I make sure he understands how the category of "snack" contains many different possibilities. I believe all parents do this instinctually but I force myself to become more conscious of my child's ability to be specific in his communications.

Starting with the most general vocabulary and working our way into the exact is a daily task. The broad must be learned first. There is no sense talking about carrots before your child knows carrots are food. Once learned, my child moves on to an understanding of how cooked carrots, raw carrots, mashed carrots, and carrot soup look and taste. Like opening the door to a whole new world of things to discover, the categories help him sort through his thoughts.

Similarly, using specific names for things makes it easier for my child to follow directions. "Find your boot" has a different meaning from "Find your shoe". If the activity I have planned for us requires specific footwear, he must learn the distinction. He has to listen to me carefully as visual clues around him may not help much. Words representing the categories he knows are often too broad for the task I need him to do. I intentionally use my words to tell him what I want without gesturing to see what he knows. If he hesitates or acts frustrated, I show him what I mean.

Although I am sure he understands "ball" as it is still one of his favorite words, there are so many balls in his collection I work on exposing him to the differences between the soccer ball, the baseball, the rubber ball and the bouncy ball. How are they all alike and how are they different? If I say to him, "We need your bouncy ball to roll down this ramp", then he knows exactly which ball to get. It must be small enough to roll down the track in order to experiment with the incline we've built on the playroom floor. I see him thinking through all his options: a soccer ball is too big, a baseball is too wobbly and the rubber ball is too light. I realize using the most specific words possible to express an idea will become a golden rule we will both need to remember.

My child loves to look at books on a topic and explore all the variety within. We have books about planets, monkeys, rocks, trucks and all subjects that might interest him. Books are another great tool for teaching different aspects of a topic and the categories for classifying things. He is learning how we organize information in books to simplify the learning process. Books become a resource for information on any topic engaging his imagination. I know whatever sparks his interest during an afternoon at the park or during playtime at home, I can get a book to refresh the memory, helping him learn more about it.

One of his favorite words, "tree" we explore further by gathering leaves from along the forest path. He discovers their shape and color differences. Later, we sit together and match them to images in a book. I share with him the names of trees according to their leaves just to show how these differences can be named. "Feel how the Spruce tree needles prickle your skin! The Beech tree leaves have one simple point at the top and the leaf with a wavy curved edge is from a Sessile Oak tree. These leaves are from different trees!" The next time we go on a walk, he looks more closely at the trees along the way and points to fallen leaves on the ground. As he grows older, I can teach him to say the names of trees and to identify them by shape. For now, knowing there is a difference is enough.

"Water" is both a favorite word and an interesting category

for my child. Are there different types of water? Bathwater, drinking water, and rainwater are three I can think of. I teach him the differences when I instruct him, "Don't drink your bathwater!" and "You shouldn't stick your hand in your cup because that water is for drinking." As he opens his mouth to catch raindrops from dark clouds overhead, I tell him, "Rainwater helps the plants grow." It would take many drops to quench his thirst with this type of water, yet he can't resist sampling what plants need to survive. Early in my childhood, I remember my first trip to the lake. With the only words I knew, I described the big blue expanse before me as, "Big water!" In our book collection, places of "big water" are a popular settings for stories, giving my child new words to learn. Oceans, lakes and rivers are now words associated with water. I enjoy helping him look more carefully at the world around him and teaching him how to learn from books.

I try to focus on identifying the words my child understands and don't fret much about his ability to say them. I know he must learn the meaning of a word before he attempts to say it. Sometimes a general word like "truck" is good enough but when he needs something more specific, I help him learn it. He will need to know when more specific words are needed. I am anxious to hear my child talk but I must remember he is listening intently all the time.

Mothers of young children complain they miss "adult conversation" when they are at home all day. It can be a challenge to talk to someone when they don't reciprocate. Our nature is to engage each other through language but if you look carefully, you will notice your child responding even in the slightest way, with attentive eyes, cooing, or hand waving. If your child is playing, he or she may pause or stop moving for a moment. Sometimes, my child lets me know he's listening by reaching out and looking directly at the source of the sound. All are good signs of a child actively listening. Keep up the good work. Your child will benefit from your diligence.

5

Nurturing Young Children with CIs

Parents, you are the key facilitators of early intervention. You must choose whether you want your child to hear with hearing aids, cochlear implant(s) and/or rely on sign language to communicate. One way or another, a child will follow the path set forth for them by their parents. From that position, you will raise and nurture your child. Your family life will be affected by your choices. The first tool parents have at their disposal to help make decisions for their child is the newborn hearing screening. Designed to identify hearing loss as early as possible in a child's life, the test provides a rapid response that is crucial for successful treatment. The later a child has access to hearing aids, cochlear implants, and speech therapy, the more his or her potential for listening and learning spoken language is at risk. Parents must know with absolute certainty the type and amount of hearing loss their child has. Given that information and within the options available, family life will accommodate hearing loss.

When parents choose cochlear implant technology, they need to realize it involves daily management of their child's speech processor and microphone. Since their first birthdays, my children have worn equipment for hearing from the time they dress in the morning until their heads hit the pillow at night. Their speech processors are protected by fanny packs at the waist and attached to a magnetic microphone by a cable. A baby can't yet know the value of the hearing equipment in his or her possession. Therefore, caretakers shoulder the responsibility. No matter what design the cochlear implant equipment has, parents of young children are accountable for its maintenance.

My husband and I make sure our children's equipment is on and working constantly. How can I expect them to listen and speak if I do not help with this simple chore? I know my children's hearing equipment must be a vital part of their daily experience, a natural and necessary extension of the body, an indispensible tool they will come to appreciate and even treasure. Parents must show their child how to take care of the equipment. It must be well cared for like hands that are clean and hair that is combed. I nurture my children best when I take responsibility for supporting the use of their cochlear implants every single day.

Living your life. With newborn hearing screenings identifying children with hearing loss earlier, a growing number of infants with cochlear implants are out with their families. The technology enables children to hear from strollers, backpack carriers, and car seats-- any place where babies are found. Parents expose them naturally to typical early childhood experiences and encourage them to discover the world as only an infant does. As they grow, families want their little ones to take part in all the activities young children enjoy. Participating in neighborhood daycares, nurseries, Sunday schools, playgroups, and music classes, toddlers with bionic ears lead busy lives. Exposure to the sounds and language of their peers is especially helpful for socialization. No matter what activities fill the calendar, good listening is key to learning in the early phases of life. From Christmas carols sung at the candlelight service to fireworks after a Fourth of July picnic, these kids are everywhere, taking it all in. The upsurge of little people seen all over with cochlear implants reflects the determination of parents who believe the audible pleasures of early childhood are well worth working for.

There are challenges to caring for a child's hearing equipment. Hearing aids are difficult to keep on tiny ears. I remember the anguish of tracking down my child's lost hearing aids with my husband at a shopping mall and along sidewalks of our well-worn path to the park. Unbeknownst to us, he had managed to flick the hearing aid off while riding in his stroller. We listened for its familiar high-pitched whine, which led us back to the missing hearing aid hidden under a bench or in the grass. The squeal also acted as alarm for an ill-fitting hearing aid mold or one pulled out of place. I resented its abrupt whine when I hugged my squirming out-of-sorts child to calm him down. After months of constantly reordering larger hearing aid ear molds to keep up with the growth of my child, I appreciated the simple design of his cochlear implant equipment. Amazingly, everything he received after the surgery can be worn for the remainder of his life. Even with new designs for his external equipment, I am glad to know the internal implant can serve him equally well in the future.

Embracing the technology. During the first few months my son wore his cochlear implant equipment, he was not self aware enough to notice. Then one day, he discovered something strapped to his middle worth investigating. Yanking the microphone from its place, he popped it in his mouth to sooth sore gums. I wonder if engineers have tested the microphone's resistance to saliva and chewing! My son certainly enjoyed experimenting with its durability. The microphone has a protective cap made of plastic covering its internal workings. As a reminder of this period, we have a collection of caps with tiny teeth marks marring the surface.

An unattached microphone can also be played with. I remember waiting in a hotel lobby with my little one impatiently sitting in his carriage. In a flash, he managed to remove his microphone from the cable surveying the room and all its opulent glory. I watched in horror as he proceeded to toss his microphone in the air. It landed squarely with a splash in the lobby's ornate fountain. If the microphone is already disposed of, my child found the end of the cable to be an adequate chew toy as well. Chewing does serious damage to the cable, as its prongs will no longer connect snugly into the microphone. Many cables later, he has abandoned this habit. Now, we always bring spare parts when traveling any distance from home.

My son adjusted to wearing the cochlear implant equipment as only a toddler could. He was too young to remember life before the surgery. With newfound kinesthetic awareness, he spent much of his time investigating how his body works, including his "mechanical" parts. His cochlear implant equipment was subjected to rigorous wear and tear, testing the limits of durability and water resistance. A power hungry tot, my son discovered he could remove the microphone for his cochlear implant. With one quick motion he knocked it down where it lay attached to the cable along the collar of his shirt. His interest in listening for the moment was not as important as his control over a situation. I would always help him put the microphone back on. Just to be sure, I checked his equipment and found everything to be working so I knew he just was experimenting.

Later on, at the preschool he attended, a fire truck parked on site as part of a lesson on community helpers. In a dramatic finale to the day's events, the firemen turned on the truck's siren and flashing lights. My son, totally engaged in the activity, wasted no time in knocking his microphone off to stop the alarming noise. I could see by the expression on his face- wide eyes and wrinkled brow- he was startled. Although the sound was unpleasant, I would make sure he would learn the siren's blare is a necessary warning or signal of danger. Riding in the car, he would eventually point when fire engines, ambulances and police cars wiz by with lights flashing and sirens blaring. Not only would he keep his microphone on and *listen*, he would know where the sound came from to understand how best to react. Sound is not to be feared. It helps him stay safe.

Hearing as much as possible. I nurtured my son through this phase by encouraging him to hear all the time. If he knocked his microphone off and we were at home, I played a children's video knowing he would want to hear the familiar songs and voices of his favorite characters. He could see them in action on the TV screen and knew they were doing something interesting. I also took him to the kitchen where I lined four cooking pots on the floor so he could "play" them with a wooden spoon. I knew he loved to hear the ringing sound and wouldn't object when I put the microphone back on. There were many sounds I knew he enjoyed hearing. I am thankful for those sounds. They enabled me to reengage him with the hearing world in a positive affirming way. It was a perplexing development, as the "window of opportunity" for acquiring the speech and language of his peers was closing as each day passed. When he wasn't able to hear, progress couldn't be made. I didn't want to battle with him about wearing his equipment or be extremely forceful either. I knew young children do not always make good choices for themselves. My job as a parent is to make those choices for him, to eat healthy foods, to get enough sleep and to see the value in books whether he wants to or not. Yet I wondered, "Why doesn't he want to hear, even if a sound is too loud or harsh? Isn't he interested in hearing everything, exploring the capacity of his senses?" I realized he responded to sudden noises in a way that protects him, like shutting one's eyes in response to a bright light. The hearing world is unable to turn off unpleasant sounds and is forced to bear them.

Considering his age, I know now he was just expressing a natural instinct to control his world, like refusing to eat dinner or get out of the bath. In a similar way, my child knocked off his microphone in times of transition or uncertainty. Riding in the car with me all over town, he enjoyed our outings together. However, I noticed he often knocked his microphone off as I lifted him out of his car seat when we arrived at our destination. Something about not knowing where we were going and what it would mean for him made my child unsettled. He was just trying to cope with things that were out of his control. Eventually, he stopped knocking the microphone off all together. There was nothing wrong with his cochlear implant.

While caring for my children, I nurtured their appreciation of sound and explained the meanings of things they heard as situations arose. I patiently helped them keep their equipment on and made sure it was working. Raising each child has been a unique experience. My daughter never went through a "resisting" phase, always leaving her microphone on as a young child. She may have been influenced by her older brother, who by that point never wanted to be without his microphone and speech processor. However, both will always have the power to turn off the sounds around them. Cochlear implant technology gives them ultimate control over their hearing. Once, I overheard a group of children remark how fun it would be to have the ability to turn their hearing on and off. I hope mine learn to appreciate the benefits of such an unusual gift.

Key Points to Consider

1. It is your responsibility to manage your child's cochlear implant.

2. Help your child wear their speech processor and microphone.

3. Take care of the technology so your child can hear as much as possible.

6

My First Year Journal: Quicker Responses

One year and six months old.

Six months with the implant.

*Six months post-surgery, my child not only learns the
meanings of new words more quickly but also reacts faster to
the ones he already knows. He responds immediately to noises
and when they startle him. He looks to the learned direction of
their source: to the sky for the roar of a jet, to the street for the
screech of a bus, and to the playground for the squeal of a
swing. His young mind reacts more accurately to sounds,
differentiating those in the environment from speech. He is
learning which sounds mean mommy's talking even when he
can't see me. I call out from another room to see how far away*

he can pick up the blended sounds of his name. He easily identifies the source of sounds but will now choose to ignore some like the quiet purr of our dishwasher in the evenings.

My child's ability to localize sound increases: his awareness of interesting things, his connection to the world, and his ability to stay safe. Before cochlear implants, children with profound hearing loss were not able to localize well enough to develop these skills fully, if at all. My child is learning to react to specific sounds in the environment and he is processing them constantly. A delayed response to sound means he might not get to see the classic Harley Davidson with shiny chrome and leather fringe rumbling down the highway. A sight he would not want to miss. Environmental sounds enrich our experiences. Sitting at the park, I close my eyes and concentrate on the rustling of leaves, the thumping of feet running from one piece of equipment to the next, the occasional cry or laugh of a child, and the bird's response to this invasion of their space. The symphony of sounds heightens my experience of the park and I hope my child will be able to fully share in them with me.

The speed at which he is able to hear with his cochlear implant defines my child's understanding of the world from a sound perspective not just a visual one. For all parents, being able to self-monitor the environment and stay safe has huge meaning. Much of my time is spent drawing my child's awareness to sounds that could impact his well-being: car engines humming in the parking lot, doors slamming shut, and most importantly the sound of his name delivered in an abrupt manner. He will learn through consequence a sharp tone of voice means "pay attention". The speed at which my child is able to perceive a sound and then know it's meaning will determine how well he can process information and use it to work, play and learn.

I can tell my child is able to understand my words faster because he pays close attention to my speech when I pronounce words for him, especially when I repeat a new sound over and over. This helps him to learn nouns, adding to his list of favorite words. As I review the latest additions to my journal, I note that many are associated with meal time and our family routine: chair, bath, clean-up, wipe, tissue, paper, cup, lid, outside, nite-nite, sleep, and baby. I continue to check the speed of his receptive language or his ability to quickly understand words naturally through play. Not only do I ask him, "What does a cow say?" but I now also include the question, "What animal says moo?" to see if he can understand converse concepts. His interaction with me is more engaged and his attempts to dialogue are so rewarding. He shakes his head when he knows something is wrong when I say, "The duck says moo!" or when I scold him for misbehaving, "Should you pour your milk on the plate?" In this way, he demonstrates his ability to not only understand language but also become an active participant in the conversation.

Understanding the word "chair" gives my child a chance to move up in the world- literally. Sitting upright is one of the most significant milestones of early childhood development. Sitting in a chair means you are civilized. My child knows things happen when someone's sitting in a chair. He observes grownups performing tasks all day long - working at the computer, paying bills, reading, eating, and watching TV. There is a powerful motivation for a small child to get up in a chair. By climbing into his highchair, my child knows there's a good chance he will be fed. To do so takes quite a bit of motivation and physical coordination. Toppling out of chairs is just an occupational hazard.

In our home, the story time chair must have good reading light with comfortable cushions. The club chairs across from the TV have room enough for he and I to cuddle. A chair at the dining table is not just a sign of mealtimes. We paint pictures, play games, do puzzles and make crafts seated at those chairs. My child makes himself busy pushing chairs around, lining them up in a row and covering them with blankets to make a fort. Since the home is a big part of my child's life every day, he quickly learns the meaning of the word "chair".

I now recognize my child understands many other common nouns, such as: "tissue", "paper", "cup", and "lid". Words often used in our daily routine are easy to teach. I ask him to give me his "cup" or a "tissue" from the many things around him, testing his comprehension without much effort. "Paper" is an especially important material he uses for all sorts of creative endeavors. Most often, paper gives him a place to draw or

*paint, to learn about color and shapes. It can also be ripped
and cut, folded and taped. Unlimited possibilities abound with
paper. I understand why these words are important to my child
and why he would need to learn them. I also am growing more
skilled at helping him become familiar with words through
repetition in our play and introducing new words that are
related to those he already knows, from "tissue" to "napkin".*

*The word "outside" suggests everything beyond the safety of
home. Exciting for my child, yet a little overwhelming, our
daily trips into the city center give him the opportunity to
study all kinds of people and things, including language and
environmental sounds. I tell him, we are going "outside" and
he knows he will have little control over what happens next.
However, I think he realizes we must go outside, venturing
from the familiar to the unfamiliar since his favorite park with
swings is outside, soccer balls are only kicked outside, and
airplanes fly outside. He eagerly gets dressed for outdoor
activity. The volatility of "outside" helps him learn to adapt to
unpredictable conditions.*

*Being outside means sharpening his awareness of
surroundings, paying closer attention to changes in the
environment. Caught in the rain, we huddle under a storefront
and chat with other patrons delayed from the next task on
their to-do list. He giggles as a raindrop hits his cheek and
listens to the patter of falling rain growing louder against the
awning. He watches the wind whipping drops of water in all
directions as they hit the cobblestone street. At night, I watch
him sleeping soundly amongst a bevy of soft animals. I
imagine him reliving his experiences, both sights and sounds
of the "outside" in beautiful vivid dreams.*

*My child recognizes people come in different sizes and he
has learned the word "baby" refers to the littlest of our kind.
When he sees a baby riding in a carriage, sitting in a high
chair, or on mother's lap he points with great enthusiasm. It's
like he's saying, "Look, there's someone like me". Reading
picture books together, he finds images of babies doing all
sorts of things: taking a bath, playing in the sandbox, or
eating small pieces of banana. Watching videos, he laughs
when babies appear as comic relief. Looking in the mirror, he
sees the reflection of his face. He studies his features just as he*

has learned to recognize mine. I suppose he realizes big people are capable of doing lots of interesting things and he is learning to call upon them for help. He knows "baby" is part of his identity.

"Clean-up" is a concept well known to my child. I constantly attend to messes made around the home as he watches. Sweeping, washing, straightening, folding, sorting, vacuuming, and stacking- so many verbs to learn by observation. He responds to the word "wipe" as I use a cloth to clean his hands or high chair tray. I teach him to help me clean up and we work together to keep our home tidy. Evidence of a good day together means a long and colorful trail of messes: toys left over from playtime, dirt tracked in from the garden, carrot tops and onionskins from cooking dinner, dishes and silverware from mealtime, and crayons strewn across the table from art projects. "Clean-up" is so central to a young child's life not much can be achieved without the need to reorder things the way they originally were. It is a cyclical part of the creative process, beginning with a blank canvas or a fresh start, enduring a burst of activity and ending with a return to order, awaiting a new inspiration. My child understands "clean-up" as it applies to all things as we have organized them in the kingdom of our home.

One of my child's most treasured times of the day is "bath" time. "Are you ready for a bath?" I ask him, as I know he looks forward to this ritual. "Bath" means at least half an hour of playing with water, discovering new ways to pour, splash, drip, float, and sink items of every material. During his bath, my child makes himself busy learning all about the element of water. I look for new objects around the house he could use to experiment with in the soapy suds. I throw a couple of ice cubes in and he smiles with surprise. Soap is not as important for washing dirt away as it is a source of bubbles to pile on his arms and toys. Actual washing is more of a distraction so I let him soak long enough to make sure his fingernails are clean. Understanding the word "bath" as an activity instead of an object is significant for my child. It is not just the white porcelain tub, silver faucet, water or soap that make a bath special for him. Hours spent in the bath help him understand our close connection with water.

The end of each day comes to a close with the words "nite-nite" and time to go to "sleep". My child must transition from activity into rest. He is aware of the light dimming outside as our evening routine allows his body to wind down and prepare for sleep. He will sometimes resist when I use the words "nite-nite". I know he understands me but in an act of defiance will not move to stop, engrossed in his play. It is exciting to know he recognizes words but has developed the ability to reason and decide for himself how he wishes to react. Providing activities he enjoys as part of his evening routine helps the inevitable come to pass.

It's been difficult to monitor how quickly my child comprehends new words. He is not speaking much yet. However, I do see him reacting rapidly to a situation when he understands what I'm saying. I must celebrate small achievements and focus on finding the items or activities of interest to continue teaching him. The cochlear implant technology processes sound quickly, allowing him to follow a conversation as it happens and to continue learning language naturally. To make this happen, I take my child to the audiologist regularly for programming and work with him at home, playing together. I have noticed a new ability to detect how the subtleties of sound induce humor. He laughs at funny noises and I revel in the joy I can share with him. I hope it is as satisfying for him to hear and acquiring language as it is for me to be participating in this amazing journey alongside him.

7

Time Without Sound

The cochlear implant's limitations are most evident when normal life circumstances require my children to remove their hearing equipment, returning them to a world of silence. A dependence on hearing mechanics creates a different reality than for those who hear all the time. Imagine what it's like to control the amount you hear from sporadic surround sound to complete quiet. Similar to closing one's eyes and letting a field of darkness replace bright colors and shapes, my children have the ability to disconnect their access to sound whenever they want. A simple magnetic force holds their microphone to the implant, making it easy to connect and disconnect their hearing. In this way, we control the equipment they wear and whether they can hear or not.

Even though my children have completely acclimated to listening with their cochlear implants, living without sound is part of their daily experience. When sleeping or showering, they always remove their speech processor and microphone to protect it from moisture damage. In other unavoidable situations, their hearing equipment could be put at risk by static electricity, magnetic force, or hard impact. We live our family life accommodating a different form of hearing and do the best we can to prioritize meaningful experiences, while avoiding situations where their equipment could be jeopardized. Parents have the primary responsibility of deciding when to take the equipment off and when to put it on if children are too young to manage.

Calculating risks. As my children's caretaker, I constantly evaluate the risks in removing their cochlear implant equipment knowing they will benefit the most if they wear it all of the time. Raising active children, I have to be careful. When my son was young, he wanted to play on a climbing structure at the playground, so he grabbed the metal bars and began his ascent. At the top, he took in the view and sank through the gap, hooking his feet around the bar. Swinging upside down, he called to me and waved. Walking closer, I noticed the cable for his cochlear implant sticking out of his shirt collar. The microphone was gone! We spent the remainder of our playtime retracing his steps, tracking down the missing piece, eventually finding it stuck to a metal bar. The powerful magnetic hold kept it hidden from plain view. Not only was the potential loss of his microphone a financial one, but my son would also have lost his hearing temporarily without it. The cochlear implant has a design contingent upon interdependent parts so all pieces must be guarded carefully.

Because my children remove their cochlear implant equipment before going to sleep every night, they do not hear upon waking in the morning or just before falling asleep. If I need to tell them something as they wake, then I put the microphone on before doing so. Likewise, if I want to say a few words of comfort before they sleep, then I do it with their equipment still on. I safeguard my children's safety while they sleep. Any tossing and turning during the night causes the microphone to fall off. Therefore, my children's fanny packs with speech processors, cables and microphones are tucked safely inside their nightstands. Their rechargeable batteries charge during the night to be ready for morning. My children are usually prepared to remove their equipment at night. They are used to sleeping in total silence. Sleepovers are a rite of passage for children old enough to venture away from home. I must trust another family completely to let my children stay the night. I know they are most likely not used to dealing with a child who wears a cochlear implant to hear or one that does not hear at night. At a recent overnight, my son woke to find himself alone as he had not heard the other children rising and racing downstairs for breakfast. I always make sure parents know my children need to be woken in the event of an emergency and told how to proceed safely. Thinking ahead and preparing the adults who will be supervising my children are important steps in keeping them safe on an overnight.

Getting the message across. If my children's equipment is off at night or for an activity like swimming, then I must consider the best way to get my message across if I need to. Sometimes a gentle hug or if there is enough light-- a smile is enough. I always increase my eye contact and touch to reassure my children. Like a second language, my non-verbal methods of communication are never as effortless as my speech but they often work to relay my feelings. My children have learned to lip-read very well, with their solid knowledge of language and watching my mouth carefully. When they are not wearing their speech processors, they only have difficulty with people who will not slow down or face them as they speak; those who don't know or forget how the world is different for them.

I think of the weekend my husband and I spent at our landlord's cabin in the Czech Republic countryside with only a pocket dictionary to facilitate the conversation. Dialogue was animated but limited to what we could manage to act out and express in a very brief number of words. I know my children have to make adjustments if they cannot hear by paying close attention to what is going on around them. They may make inferences based on past experience or use intuition. My children are so integrated into the hearing world that they want to hear as much as possible.

Living with cochlear implant technology means deciding

what's best for our children in situations that naturally occur. When the microphone is covered by a helmet, hat, or under a costume, ordinary circumstances interfere with hearing. Baseball hats rubbing on my son's microphone affect the quality of sounds he hears so we bring a sun umbrella for the beach. We have searched for comfortable helmets to go on family bike rides. I alter Halloween costumes with a hat or crown to accommodate the microphone and not obstruct my children's hearing. I want them to wear the costumes of their choice, expressing their personality and interests regardless of the cochlear implant equipment.

Pool time presents a unique set of challenges. Learning to swim requires "dry land" lessons or learning by observation. Pool parties involve games and water sports with limited but crucial spoken communication. My children love to swim but sometimes find it too challenging to keep up with the conversations. People often forget or don't understand why they are not responding in the pool, especially when they are used to them speaking and listening so naturally. I have learned to let my children decide when to participate in water activities and they now assert their own opinions. A few years ago, while visiting a theme park, my son watched and waited as a friend spun on a whirling water ride. Suddenly the thrill of swinging through random sprays of water was too much to resist. He decided to take a turn. I held his fanny pack to keep it dry so he could accompany his friend once more on the ride. Back at my side, we quickly refastened it under his water splattered t-shirt while he chattered away. An important developmental step for my children has been becoming accountable for their own cochlear implant equipment.

Evaluate the tradeoffs. After watching many people interact with my children, I am both excited and frustrated by what I have experienced. Those who know them are accustomed to their natural reaction to sound. They do not anticipate when an activity might prevent them from wearing their equipment and how it may limit their interaction with peers. They do not consider what it means for us, having to decide whether our children participate by removing their access to language or sit on the sidelines, hearing all but not experiencing what life is offering at that moment.

Deciding when my children should hear and when to remove the equipment is an interesting quandary. It's difficult to avoid being caught in the rain so is it better just to bring a waterproof bag to put the equipment in or bring a hat? At the beach, is it more important to hear the sound of the surf or run in the waves? Either choice is a trade off. I try to make sure my children experience the world with all of their senses.

The best solution is to follow my children's lead and help them manage to keep the equipment safe. Especially, when their hearing depends entirely on all components of the cochlear implant functioning perfectly. The cost to replace cochlear implant equipment is reason enough to protect it from humidity and other environmental factors. If the microphone, cable or speech processor break, we contact the manufacturer and have new components sent to us by mail. Meanwhile, my child cannot hear. Since the external equipment cannot easily be replaced, I consider the risks carefully before letting my children go for any length of time without hearing. Cochlear implant companies are becoming aware of the tough decisions parents face and are now offering smaller more waterproof products. The future will certainly bring improved designs solving many of these issues.

Key Points to Consider

1. Consider the impact on your child when pieces of their hearing equipment are lost or broken.

2. Communicate even when your child can't hear.

3. Evaluate the tradeoffs when removing your child's speech processor and microphone for an activity.

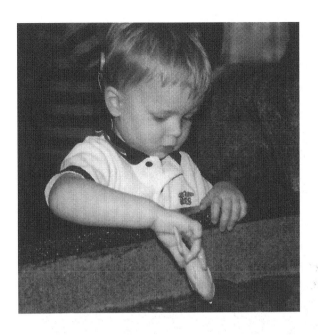

8

My First Year Journal: Understanding More

One year and seven months old.

Seven months with the implant.

At seven months with the implant, my child's understanding of language has grown tremendously. I know because of the way he reacts to my questions. He knows I am waiting for a response. Even when he gestures with his hands for something, he verbalizes. Not satisfied just understanding words, he wants to say them. If his hands are covered with glue, he declares, "Dirty!" He knows the word is expected. I continue encouraging him to learn the meaning of new words through play, especially those that might help him express his feelings better. Even though he understands many words, he may feel frustrated by not being able to communicate all of his thoughts verbally. The struggle will motivate him to listen more carefully to what I say. He now understands how to acquire new words and I am convinced he has learned many more on his own. My job is now to be aware of what he is interested in and follow his lead. I add 86 new words to my vocabulary journal under the heading "expressive language" to differentiate them from "receptive language" or words he understands but does not yet say.

The majority of words in my journal are nouns and I wonder if it's easier for him to learn the names of concrete objects – things he can take into hand, exploring their texture, color and weight. They are items mostly found in our home, things he has become familiar with by learning their role in our lives. Books from the Richard Scarry series help us review the new nouns in his repertoire. Playing "I Spy", I ask him to find an object hidden among many on the page. He sits next to me or on my lap and does not look at my face. He is too intent on finding the object in question. I am reassured of many things: his cochlear implant is working, his listening skills are improving, he understands what I am expecting of him, and he identifies the correct object when he's able. Best of all, these actions are happening more quickly than ever before. The possibilities for introducing nouns are endless and I talk to him as I work, describing what I am doing in great detail. Luckily, I have a very keen observer whose eyes follow me everywhere I go.

My child's knowledge of verbs stems from the actions he performs every day. Most are one syllable: "eat", "kick", and "spin". The act of doing something instead of just learning about it from a safe distance makes a big impression on his memory. Using all his senses, my child draws information from a situation. In the morning, my child loves to eat hot cereal. Warm and filling, he has become very at good spooning small bites into his mouth. Not only an effective practice of the word "eat", I view it as another major step towards independence! I ask him, "Do you want to eat some hot cereal?" He watches as I take milk from the fridge, put it on the stove to warm up, slowly pour in the grains and stir until thick. Right now "eat" means many things to my child. "Eat" means hungry. "Eat" means mom prepares food. "Eat" means sitting together at the table. "Eat" means a chance to enjoy favorite foods as well as taste new flavors and experience new textures. We have many opportunities to practice the word "eat" together.

As soon as my child learned to "kick", he began to move balls around with his feet encouraged by my husband. There are endless ways to use the word "kick" in play: "kick it harder", "kick it higher", "kick it back to me", "kick it up the hill", "kick it into the goal", and with a little bit of training "kick it over the bush". Just like the hours of practice needed to master the footwork to kick, my child works constantly on understanding all the different ways "kick" is used as an action word in my sentences. Just to emphasize the meaning, I say the word "kick" directly as he makes contact with the ball, sending it up the hill in front of our house before rolling back down again for another turn. Once I'm sure he knows what "kick" means, I can check his understanding of instructions by telling him where to direct the ball. There are many actions words I practice with him, such as "throw", "hit", "roll", "pull", and "slide" by saying the word as he acts it out.

He is also learning adjectives. "Hot" is a favorite word to describe the sensation electrifying his tiny fingers or lips. His appetite for hot cereal could be partly due to the cold, dark mornings in Germany, where waking up to a chilly floor can be remedied with a chamomile tea or bowl of hot cereal. Bath time is not only good for soaking dirt from between the toes but also to experiment with temperature. Finding the optimal warmth is key to relaxing before bedtime. Too hot is unpleasant for delicate skin so my child carefully dips his small finger into the swirling bath water, watching it turn pink. Too cold and his finger responds with a disagreeable pucker. There will be no bath unless the water meets his specifications. He lets me know if I come too close with my hairdryer afterwards. I tease him with bursts of hot air on his back. Later, I fold "hot" laundry from the dryer, rapping my child snuggly in a fresh sheet. It can be "hot" outside and "hot" in the oven. As an adjective, "hot" changes a noun in a drastic way and my child takes notice.

I know my child already understands a few adverbs of place, describing the location of something familiar. He is keenly aware of the significant people in his life and likes to keep

*track of where they are. I ask him, "Is Papa outside?" He runs
to the door and peers through the side window at the driveway
out front. Watching his father's car turn into the driveway, my
child knows "outside" means beyond the limits of our home.
Sitting at the table one morning, we watch the light push the
shadows from our garden. I see movement near the hedge
through the patio door initiated by an orange and white
flicker of fur. "Look at the fox outside!" My child jumps on my
lap, startled by the prospect of wild creatures "outside" our
safe haven. We watch the fox glance around clearly displaced
from its territory before bolting between the trees. My child
finds the world outside both fascinating and unpredictable.*

*Another beloved adverb is "up". When you are small,
everything worth having is "up", just out of reach. Tables,
counters, shelves all have books and interesting trinkets above
a small child's line of vision. In fact, to the young mind
anything out of reach is highly suspect and worthy of
investigation. My child is certain he needs to get "up" there
somehow. Tired from a daily dose of walking, my child reaches
with outstretched arms demanding "up". As I lift him to my
hip, he settles in satisfied with his new vantage point.
Likewise, he tugs my hand as I sit on the floor of the playroom
with urgency where "up" means get up, let's go or move it
mom. Outside "up" might refer to what he observes in the
treetops or to the birds and airplanes passing overhead. We
release a balloon and watch it float lazily "up" into the clouds.
My child understands the word "up" indicates the direction of
an action: looking, jumping, or throwing.*

*My child loves hiding games so it's easy to practice the word
"inside" with his toys. He enjoys making things disappear from
view, clearly pleased by the illusion. Gone but not gone, the toy
is hidden inside something. He closes his eyes as I place a
small plastic tiger inside a box. When he opens his eyes, I tell
him to find the tiger. He now understands what that means
and what to do. He knows he will not be able to see the tiger
and he will have to use his tiny fingers to find openings in
things and look inside. As he moves around the room, his mind
must decide whether there is space enough inside something
to hide the toy tiger. Finally, with a shout, he pulls the tiger
from the box. Later when he is busy in the sandbox, I tell him*

it's time to go "inside". How he complains...not wanting to stop playing. I reiterate, "Let's go inside." He slowly pulls himself up and heads for the door. "Inside" means the day's worth of activities is over and it's time to wind down.

My journal helps me to be patient and celebrate the new words he has acquired during this receptive explosion. Sometimes it's hard for me to grasp how well my child is doing in his acquisition of words. I have no comparison to work from, just lists of words a child his age should understand. The journal is critical for tracking his progress. I need to respect him as an individual with unique interests driving his learning. The words in my journal can now be categorized into groups: vehicles, people, toys, foods, animals, clothes, greetings, household items, body parts, things from nature, and technology. With these classifications established I target his learning even further, building on his current word base. Once he knows a word, I continue to show him how it can be used in different circumstances. I teach him how complex our language is and he must learn to recognize the context of a word to understand the intended meaning.

I also work with my child to produce sounds that might help his speech, like blowing air through pursed lips. When I want to make him smile, I blow on his tummy. He blows back in imitation. In his room, he blows air at the stars hanging in a mobile, making them spin and swirl. Later, as we read a book together, a picture of stars prompts him to blow air at the picture. I think of other situations where he can practice blowing. During our Christmas celebrations in Germany, we light a traditional Christmas "pyramid" to mark the advent season. The painted wooden figures of children and Santa spin as hot air from four candles move propeller-like pieces. Without the candles lit, my child eagerly blows the propellers, revolving tiny statues around a miniature Christmas tree. He doesn't realize all of this blowing is actually strengthening his muscles for articulation and helping him speak clearly. We make each other laugh with other silly sounds and simply enjoy the musical quality of our voices.

I continue to attend playgroups, trying not to compare my child's speech to his peers. Some children are naturally more talkative. I watch as they actively seek the attention of others, drawing a playmate into their pursuits. Personality comes into play. Children with outgoing natures have more eye contact and are more physical and verbal with others. I am relieved in knowing there is a great variety in speech production among kids and my friends seem to believe that boys naturally talk less. My child needs more practice to express himself as confidently as his friends. I have to smile, knowing he is completely unaware of my sense of urgency. He's often more interested in manipulating his play dough or coloring a picture than speaking. I cannot force him to develop faster than he naturally will. I can only be available to him when he wants to learn. I know he relies completely on the sound reaching his implant as he understands most words without looking directly at my mouth. This represents a huge shift in behavior; he is reacting to my speech more like a hearing child than one with hearing loss. I am very excited by this rapid development and his receptive language explosion.

9

Managing Cochlear Implant Equipment

Like any mechanical device, the cochlear implant has the potential to let your child down. Even with its tremendous durability tested by daily wear and tear, the equipment will stop working when your child needs to hear. Man-made technology no matter how ingenious will break down or be damaged by exposure or overuse. Learning to be prepared for equipment failures makes you, as primary caretaker of your child's external components, a troubleshooting expert. With time, you will learn what the most common problems are and build a response plan for those situations. My children's cochlear implants have a built-in alarm to signal when a link in the chain of technology is broken, as sound travels from microphone to cable to processor to implant. If any of these components are damaged or not connected fully, the implant will not work and my children will not hear. Initially, I found the beeping noise signaling a break in the connection intrusive, a dramatic reminder of my children's dependence on the implant for hearing. I eventually learned to appreciate the certainness of an alarm in a world where I was never quite sure what my children were hearing in all types of environments and situations. It is our responsibility to keep it working at all times.

Sounding the alarm. The cochlear implant alarm is triggered most often when the microphone loses contact with the implant. Magnets in the microphone secure it on top of my children's hair to the implant's magnet just under the skin. The magnetic pull is simply not strong enough to keep the microphone in place under all circumstances. Too much magnetic force irritates the skin so the microphone is kept loosely secure. Any number of actions can knock the microphone from its place and prompt the alarm to sound: a summersault on the bed, a tender hug, a turn on the monkey bars or a ride in the car seat.

Especially for an infant who cannot control his head or must frequently lie on his back, the microphone's magnetic force is often compromised. Luckily, this problem can be quickly and easily resolved. The moment the microphone is off; an alarm alerts me my child cannot hear and I immediately pop it back into place. As soon as they were old enough, I helped them learn where their implant was located so they could reconnect the microphone by themselves. Performing this task is not only helpful to me but another sign of growing independence.

Another more demanding technological issue is the constant stream of battery power necessary to run the cochlear implant's speech processor. My children's equipment relies on regular AA rechargeable batteries. To keep up with demand, they must be recharged overnight in an electrical charger. A critical part of my children's morning routine is replacing old batteries with a set that is freshly charged each day. Early mornings at our house are no less chaotic than most. More important than finding the right outfit to wear, my children must have working batteries for their speech processors before we dash off in the car. I have made the U-turn for home to retrieve a new set of batteries more than once when the old ones suddenly stopped working. Because there is no way to tell exactly how much "juice" a battery has left, we always err on the side of caution and begin the day with newly charged batteries. With a life of around 18 hours, we have discovered is it important to have backup batteries with us at all times.

Even with the most conscientious effort, we have left activities because our children's batteries have died and we'd forgotten to bring replacements along. When my son was still a toddler, we rode the train from Milan's airport to the city center. Mid-trip his batteries died. Once at the station, we rummaged through our belongings amid a stream of travelers to find some spares. On another trip, our tour of Edinburgh Castle in Scotland was cut short by his battery failure. Not unlike other emergencies that send parents of young children running for home, unpredictability is the hardest challenge when managing cochlear implant equipment. One cannot always anticipate how long things will take and how far a child will venture from where new batteries are stored. Family life is continuously interrupted by the question, "Honey, did we bring spare batteries?"

Stress on the cable connecting the speech processor to the microphone eventually impairs the cochlear implant. My children's cables are covered by soft flexible brown plastic. One end of the wire attaches to the speech processor and the other to the microphone. They wear the thin cable under their shirts, running from the fanny pack up to the microphone behind the ear. Over time, the cable stiffens from wear and sweat, eventually causing it to harden and break. Sometimes, I can see torn metal hairs through a hole in the cable's outer coating. Other times, I can't see the break at all but my child hears a buzzing sound and is able to describe it to me. Either way, the processor is no longer able to gather clear sounds via the microphone. The serious consequence of a simple cable break has resulted in the purchase of many new cables rush-shipped to our home. They are sold in varying lengths so we double-check the size against a growing body. If the cable is too short, it will pull the microphone from its place behind the ear when my child bends over. We always have an extra cable as a backup.

Intermittent hearing. If my children's microphone is slightly disconnected from the cable or only partially inserted, then their hearing is intermittent. Inconsistent hearing caused by a technical problem may not be obvious. From a distance, the cable and microphone appear connected. Only upon close inspection will the separation be apparent. With intermittent hearing, the cochlear implant's alarm gives off a single beep instead of a continuous stream of signals. If my children are in a noisy environment an isolated sound from the implant may go unheeded. Likewise, if the other end of the cable is not fully inserted into the speech processor, hearing is affected in the same way. Both ends must be securely attached to complete the path to the hearing nerve. When the alarm sounds, I have learned to check the connection to the microphone first as even a slight separation from the cable will prevent sound from reaching the implant.

A loose or stretched cable connection also makes it easier for the microphone to fall off. If the cable is wearing out, my children's microphones will detach with the slightest tug and drop to the floor. Quite a bit more expensive to replace, I have spent serious time looking for missing microphones to avoid buying a new one. There are different colored interchangeable caps for the microphone but we always pick one to match their hair color. Brightly colored caps would certainly be easier to find then a brown one. However, my children's equipment causes enough attention without looking like a red or blue button on the side of the head.

One day out on the playground, a well-known bully decided to grab my son's microphone in a surprise attack from behind. Was it out of curiosity or malice? Either way, the microphone detached from the cable and the child threw it in haste as high as he could. The playground was covered with small brown woodchips, exactly the same shade as his microphone cap. A search ensued and the microphone was eventually found. Amazingly, the child who misbehaved did not receive consequences for his actions, as the aftercare staff had no idea what the microphone was for. They did not understand how critical the equipment was for my son's hearing because he continued to speak and interact with them even when he could not hear. The microphone, exactly the size of a half dollar coin, has critical value as an external component of the cochlear implant so we have a spare to cover emergencies.

Prioritize audiology appointments. Every visit to the audiologist includes an appraisal of my children's cochlear implant equipment. We have dealt with many other equipment issues, just much less frequently. My children know to slide the battery case securely into the speech processor for a good connection. A slight crack in the plastic case prevents the battery power from properly charging the speech processor. Securing the pack tightly with a rubber band solves the problem temporarily. Eventually, we must buy a new battery case to eliminate the problem. Although unlikely, water or humidity seeping through the tiny opening in the microphone causes moisture damage to internal components. We find a thin layer of plastic wrap is effective in protecting it at the beach. The cable joint to the speech processor is vulnerable as body movement pulls upward, straining the wire inside. Each part of the external equipment must be fully connected and in good working order to provide a young child with constant hearing. In addition, we come to audiology appointments prepared to report any changes or preferences when hearing with the implant, including my own observations to help the audiologist in programming in speech processor.

Parents are initially accountable for taking care of their infant's cochlear implant equipment. Upon making the choice to give their child access to hearing, parents have to keep the device operating properly and be sure it is worn constantly. There are no breaks and no exceptions to this commitment. Without continuous access to sound, a child will not receive the maximum benefit from their cochlear implant.

Eventually, the youngster learns to take over the responsibility. This includes replacing his or her own batteries each morning, snapping fanny packs around the waist, snaking the cable up the back of the shirt, placing the microphone atop the implant, and finally turning the speech processor to the correct program. Children who use other cochlear implant designs such as the "BTE" or Behind the Ear model have similar responsibilities. If the alarm goes off or the device is not working, batteries, cables and all connections must be checked.

When we are not together, my children are responsible for

their cochlear implant equipment while at school, during sleepovers, and at camp. They must alert an adult for help if they need it. For my children to hear friends, participate in activities, follow directions and keep safe, their external equipment must be working. The cochlear implant is a technological miracle for those who want to live in the hearing world, so its mechanical limitations although sometimes inconvenient are simply worth the extra precaution.

Key Points to Consider

1. The alarm signals your child's cochlear implant is not working.

2. A damaged cable or microphone causes intermittent hearing.

3. Prioritize and prepare for your child's audiology appointments.

10

My First Year Journal: Your Turn to Talk

One year and eight months old.

Eight months with the implant.

My child is very interested in learning to speak, as he now understands much of what is being said to him, if only in pieces. His receptive language is growing to an unrecognizable scope. I record notable progress in my journal to keep focused and help him in his quest for language. I settled into my role as chatty mommy, providing lively descriptions of life around us. His awareness of language, both receptive and expressive, is heightened. I am still apprehensive of his future and can only hope our efforts will be justified. Even at this point in our progress, no doctor or therapist assures us of his conceivable potential. I hold onto my dream of one day hearing his voice tell me he loves me. There are many variables to account for: the stability of our home life, the capabilities of my child's speech therapist, in combination with his intellectual potential.

Fortunately, my husband and I are always aligned about the treatment of our child's hearing loss. We want to help him speak and listen. We believe the cochlear implant technology will enable him to hear well enough to learn language, be more engaged with his surroundings and keep him safe. We have faith in our ability to be disciplined over the course of his treatment and above all we have courage enough to risk entering into the unfamiliar territory of bionic hearing. Our optimism might seem foolish but we are no different from most parents whose enthusiasm over raising offspring skyrockets before sleeplessness, diaper rash and teething ensue.

In dealing with our child's hearing loss, like-mindedness creates a powerful driving force behind our decisions. If mother and father are not in agreement over the treatment of their child's hearing loss, then the negative impact of conflict at home will raise barriers to learning as well as stunt the child's emotional health. While difficult issues arising in a marriage should be met with lively discussion and debate, resolving differences and working together in unison greatly benefits a child. The home environment is a factor often not addressed by healthcare professionals who focus purely on a child's hearing loss, leaving parents to sort out their differences alone.

With both parents focusing on his every move, my child likes to sit with us and tell a big story, especially in the morning. His words may not all be clear yet, but he seems to understand what a story is and he enjoys our undivided attention. With expressive eyes traveling from his father's face to my own, he blinks and throws his arms up to emphasize a point. We respond with an animated, "Wow!" and "Really?" to his outbursts of baby babble peppered with his favorite words. If we can understand what he's trying to say, we make sure to help by providing the vocabulary he needs. Always pausing to give him time to respond, we banter back and forth with enthusiasm. I am excited to see this particular progress in his language development.

A story is a unique kind of expression, different than asking a question or giving a command. Telling a story requires more vocabulary and complex thinking. My child is attempting to string together more than one word/sound to express an idea. He must have observed our conversations over dinner as he nibbled on his food and as he sat in his car seat on our frequent trips to Frankfurt, noting the length and duration of our utterances during a conversation. It is humorous to see oneself reflected in a child. We teach him many things about language without even realizing it. His desire to express himself verbally is powerful and encouraging to us. Very different from his attempts to say one or two words clearly, his "stories" follow the rhythm and pattern of dialogue. Although they are not yet clearly told, we respect his need to tell them as best he can.

My child is learning to speak by repeating what I say, imitating my pronunciation of a word. This requires careful listening. I often stand behind him and slow my speech down giving him time to process my words. The implant must help him hear speech clearly, including soft and high frequency sounds. If my child responds when I say the letters: "f", "s" and "th" from where he cannot see me, I feel reassured he can hear me comfortably. However, many variables outside of my control interfere with his hearing. Background noise is particularly disrupting.

In playgroup, where contextual commotion can reach epic proportions, I watch how other children try the same methods with their mothers to learn new words and communicate their needs. I am surprised how often children are ignored when women focus on their own desire to talk with other moms about adult topics, comparing notes and releasing pent up emotion. I try to always affirm my child's efforts to speak. Perhaps, I resent how other mothers don't have to worry about what their children are saying and how well they pronounce words. It's difficult to be conscious of others taking for granted something I know my child is working hard to do. When I see him responding to my encouragement, I make an effort to show my child I'm proud of his attempts to communicate. In the long run, I know he is also getting the message his mother loves him.

Although I have not taught my child sign language, he is very animated physically when he expresses himself. He often uses hand gestures to communicate along with words. These movements emphasize what is being said. I am sure he is copying what my husband and I do with our hands as we speak without even realizing it. My child frequently points as he verbalizes to make sure I understand his intentions. He is very effective in drawing my attention to his desired wishes. I sometimes pretend I don't comprehend what he is saying to encourage him to articulate his words better. With amazing self-awareness of where the sound is entering his body, he also points at his microphone to indicate when he has heard something. As a way of saying, "I hear that", he actually helps me know his cochlear implant is working just fine. Likewise, he will point when he wants to hear something. Without always being able to put words to his thoughts, his determination to communicate is admirable.

My child is developing a genuine interest in producing sounds of his own invention. We purchase basic instruments and noisemaking toys, asking family and friends to consider musical gifts for our child. Some of these playthings became well-loved favorites. We laugh about how we let a toy Elmo's never-ending musical song and rocking body remain quiet after its batteries eventually wear out. Pre-packaged music making sets include: drums for banging on, triangles for chiming, tambourines for shaking, and gourds for rattling. My child uses them all to understand rhythm. I tap out a sequence and try to encourage him to imitate me. Not only is he able to hear the pattern but also I am impressed with his ability to produce it.

There are so many ways to experiment with musical sounds. I ask him to blow into the harmonica and he is startled yet pleased by its loud blend of sounds. We also play on a small keyboard together. As I play Twinkle, Twinkle, Little Star, he listens to me hum. The keyboard helps me introduce the difference between high and low pitches. Other toys producing sound effects captivate his attention and have the added benefit of challenging his thinking. The Wack-a-Mole game is a favorite for not only honing quick reaction skills with the hammer but also for the humorous cries of moles in peril. Our classic Farmer in the Dell pull toy helps him learn animal sounds. I am excited to have so many fun and engaging ways to help my child practice listening with popular toys of children his age.

My child is now showing preferences for certain types of formal music. I learn which songs he enjoys listening to as we sing along with characters from his favorite videos. I watch my child move his body to the rhythm of music and my heart lifts along with his. Realistically, I wasn't sure how much he would be able to enjoy music with his bionic ear. I knew from the beginning that speech and language were more important goals to focus on. However, in my heart, I want him to appreciate music as much as I do.

The cochlear implant not only gives him the ability to listen and learn language, it also gives him music. I now have proof of that fact. When we watch a little MTV, the rock stars dancing and singing in front of colorful funky graphics mesmerize him. The songs have lots of repetition and their catchy tunes are easy to learn. As I sing him to sleep, rocking slowly in the dim light, I know he can feel breath filling my lungs and can sense what joy the voice can bring through song. He understands how soft voices calm, relax, sooth and reassure just as he stiffens and winces at my raised voice. Music in all its forms has been a marvelous way for us to push the limits of his cochlear implant.

After much consideration, my husband and I decide to help our child only learn English at present. Even though I speak some German and my husband is fluent, we work to rapidly establish American English as my child's language. We want him to master English in all forms, as a speaker, reader and writer. If his language is not yet as strong as his peers, then we should focus exclusively on that goal. I am not concerned about his ability to acquire foreign languages.

With compromised hearing, we know we are reaching for something that is not easy to achieve. My husband and I agree; once he learns English, he will be able to study other languages if he so desires. Living abroad, it is not easy to limit how much German he hears. Shopping around town, chatting with neighbors, watching the local news, and visiting with doctors all expose him to German. In response, I constantly search for good sources of English. My expatriate friends and I share the latest "Barney" and "Bob the Builder" children's videos brought over from the States. While my friends use the videos as a distraction for their children, I feel good about giving my child English language programming specifically designed for preschoolers. I play these precious videos so often my husband and I know all the songs by heart. I create an English language bubble for my child by attending American playgroups, watching American movies and listening to American music. However, I never disregard my own value as an important source of language for my child.

My child must be acutely aware of what his implant does for him, as he makes sure his microphone is on for certain activities, especially when it involves individual attention from us. Reading together is still a favorite pastime for my child. When we read from our collection of his favorite books, he listens intently, trying harder to participate. Rereading books helps him to anticipate what is coming ahead in the plot by learning the language of story telling. I believe our reading time together encourages him to tell stories of his own. He understands the pleasure of stories, the lessons learned and the engaging use of language. He responds quickly when I ask him to identify objects in books, pictures, puzzles, videos and computer games. The cochlear implant is now an indispensible part of him.

11

Inclusion verses Seclusion

Being the only one with a cochlear implant may stir feelings within your child, especially when belonging is important. Singled out by academic or athletic success, my children welcome the extra attention. Yet, there are times they just want to fit in, even sacrificing their own individuality to be a part of a group. If hearing loss becomes an issue, then they must either prove they belong or stand proudly on their own. Time and again, I have seen how my children's hearing loss is uncovered in a group. At first, when their cochlear implant equipment is discreetly hidden and their speech, listening skills and behavior seem very age appropriate, they blend into the crowd. After a while, someone may notice the microphone and cable and wonder what they are for. They might observe how my children move closer to the person who is speaking, their hearing loss now exposed. Finally, they may detect how my children miss bits of information or conversation in all the noise.

Hearing loss is not common in young children. Around one baby in a thousand is diagnosed per year. Even within a family, often only one sibling will have profound hearing loss. Finding themselves alone in their uniqueness, despite mandatory newborn hearing screenings, expanded insurance coverage for cochlear implants and improved awareness of the oral option for the deaf choosing to speak, my children must be brave. We seldom see someone else with a cochlear implant in classes at school, summer camp, or on vacation. In every circumstance, their unique hearing condition influences their experience either towards inclusion or seclusion.

Finding others like you. Seeking a more inclusive environment for our children, we moved back to the States so they could attend a preschool for the deaf in Redwood City, California. Again, we were led by their needs. During a brief but important three-year period from age 2 to 5, my son spent every weekday in an environment surrounded by peers who had hearing loss. My daughter was enrolled from 6 months to 2 ½ years old. At the school, most children are battling the effects of hearing loss through therapy and practice. My husband and I befriended other parents, who reminded us that we were not the only ones grappling with a rare condition.

Inclusion is never an issue at an "oral option" school. All classroom undertakings are designed to encourage my children to listen and use their voices. Teachers understand what hearing loss means for students and how to motivate their learning process, constantly affirming their self-esteem with praise and encouragement. They know all the parts of the cochlear implant equipment and how to problem solve when they aren't working. While my children attended the school, they were never made to feel inadequate or inferior. What a relief it was for us to trust in the faculty and know they were doing their best to make sure my children felt completely accepted and included in all school activities.

Outside the sheltering walls of the "oral option" school, my children would learn to be patient with a world not familiar with their special health condition. When my son was five, he was ready to attend a regular kindergarten. After reviewing all the possibilities for mainstreaming both children, we decided on a medium-sized private school with a preschool class where we hoped a small student teacher ratio and higher academic expectations would help them succeed. I even worked as an instructor at the school to build a professional rapport with my children's teachers. Besides their sibling, they needed to feel comfortable being the only one at school with an extraordinary device for hearing. Inclusion should be natural in a culture celebrating difference but even in the United States reality can be complicated for those with hearing loss.

Children with cochlear implants are invited to mainstream in local schools through No Child Left Behind legislation, but how are they actually "included"? The teacher and classmates almost certainly will have no previous experience with someone who uses a cochlear implant to hear. Even the IEP or Individualized Education Plan used by public schools to set educational goals for children with hearing loss are not always well written or followed. Although experiences vary by location, our brief encounter with the public school IEP team actually drove us to a private school setting. Some children with cochlear implants make use of FM systems (wireless assistive listening systems) to improve hearing in loud classrooms but after three years of struggling with faculty over FM practices, our children stopped using it altogether with no real ramifications.

Inclusion at school. Working with teachers, I have tried to help my children achieve a greater level of inclusion in classroom activities, field trips, music performances and sports. I always provide materials from our cochlear implant manufacturer for the classroom, specifically written to help teachers become familiar with the needs of students with hearing loss. It's not clear to me how much these paper resources help. I believe teachers like to observe children and make their own conclusions about what kind of students they are. Teachers don't seem to worry about my children's overall experience in the classroom or their interaction with peers when they are able to follow lessons and grasp the material. I don't blame teachers and classmates for their initial lack of understanding and empathy, because they simply don't know what it's like to hear with a cochlear implant.

Although everyone in the classroom should be sensitive to the needs of individual students, I have struggled with the pros and cons of drawing more attention to my children's already singular condition. How much should teachers know about their personal health? A detailed in-service at the beginning of the school year emphasizes differences, hopefully inspiring teachers to understand how hearing loss might impact learning. I have never included my children's classmates in the in-service but can understand why some families choose to do so.

A family must decide how and when to arrange for an in-service at school. By educating teachers on my children's hearing loss, I hope to create awareness of their personal battle to hear. However, I feel aspects of their condition are private and should remain a family issue. Even after leading detailed in-services, there are still misunderstandings about the cochlear implant at school. I have found that a single teacher in-service is not enough, especially when my children were very young. To prevent teachers from being overwhelmed with huge amounts of information, it is often more effective to answer questions and solve problems as they come up. I know I will always be my children's best advocate.

Developing a close partnership with their teachers will ensure full inclusion in class. When I physically show teachers and staff the cochlear implant's external equipment, explain the battery power and technical issues my children may have during the school day, it makes a big impression. By the time I am finished, there is no way to claim ignorance in knowing what their needs are and how to assist them. We discuss where bags of spare batteries will be located around the school campus for emergencies and when to prioritize their seating to best hear a speaker. Last but not least, I discuss the potential for social misunderstandings at school; reminding them the cochlear implant does not "cure" hearing loss. I am determined not to let this fact prevent them from being fully included as students in school.

Mainstream challenges. Leaving the controlled environment of the school classroom presents another challenge for inclusion. Every field trip must be thought through in advance to anticipate barriers to hearing and participating in all planned encounters. If I do not prepare, I risk damage to their self-esteem in the event of a problem. At my children's private school, the fifth grade class travels each year to Washington, D.C. Parents are not allowed to chaperone. Even with my son's special health condition, I was told I could not travel with the group.

My husband and I decided to meet with the fifth grade team to air our concerns about his traveling alone for a week. I wanted the chaperones to have a formal plan in the event of equipment failure. In a meeting, I asked the teachers, "What would he do if his equipment broke down? Sit on the bus for hours not hearing and wait for the other children to finish a tour? Would there be enough staff to take him separately to the hotel?" The head teacher paused for a moment then suggested my son might not want to attend the annual trip. My husband retaliated with a Blitz Krieg response to her audacity. Mainstream private school is not required by law to include all children in activities and our experience has been if teachers and administration believe my child will require more work for them, participation will be discreetly discouraged.

We negotiated the terms of his travel and agreed to send our only back up device along, although the staff did not seem to understand its value. At one point, someone suggested it be stored under the bus for "safety"! We knew Washington D.C. temperatures could easily fall below freezing so we insisted it stay inside the heated bus at all times. My son enjoyed his experience in our nation's capital and felt awestruck by the sights along with his fellow classmates. However, I can't imagine how badly things would have been handled had we not sat through those tough pre-trip planning meetings.

Many social events outside of school present special challenges for my children. We now live in Florida and many parties take place at swimming pools. Summers are spent trying to stay cool and comfortable in the hot humid air. My children can choose to participate as they love to swim but in doing so they give up their access to hearing. They would rather take their equipment off, blending in with the crowd than have wires and mechanical parts hanging off their body. To my amazement, I have seen them agree to play Marco Polo, moving through the water with lighting speed, brushing against another child by accident rather than by localizing sound. Included in the games but pretending to participate, it never occurs to people nearby that my children cannot close their eyes and follow the taunting calls of those encircling them in the water.

The beach is no different, with the elements of both sand and ocean threatening to damage the equipment. Even with it tucked safely inside our beach bag, I bring it to shelter in a wet season downpour, nervous about potential damage. New waterproof cochlear implant technology allows for water play but I wonder if my children will choose to participate with fragile, visible equipment? Will it increase or decrease their inclusion in the group?

One of the most painful things my children have experienced is social isolation. In this case, they won't be physically attacked but they won't be included either. By turning away, children will sometimes ignore their attempts to participate in a conversation. A clever passive aggressive form of bullying, it leaves no physical mark but hurts deeply regardless. This behavior is often as painful as vicious words or physical harm. It's difficult to tell if the offenders are intentionally being insensitive or just focused on establishing their place in the group, confirming their rank in the social hierarchy. I know all children can become isolated from a group. However, if a physical difference or a hearing loss is the reason for not including a child, then they are victims of prejudice. The act of turning away or becoming physically distant prevents my children from hearing and therefore participating. Teachers don't always know how to address this type of behavior in their classrooms if no mark is outwardly visible.

When I found out my second child needed a cochlear implant, I knew she might be the best safeguard against my son's social isolation. Having another child in our home that needs fresh batteries, strains to hear over background noise, and sleeps in quiet silence provides true companionship to my son. Partners in crime, my children enjoy a higher level of compassion and understanding because of their cochlear implants. I want them to always find solace in their common condition. I will never be able to experience how it feels even if I try to imagine the world through a cochlear implant. When my son's frustrations overwhelm him, my daughter is there with empathetic sympathy. Over time, my son and daughter have indeed developed a special connection that has strengthened their sibling relationship.

I sense my children constantly fight to be included in a world filled with curious indifference to avoid misunderstandings. If they have trouble hearing, then they must work to resolve the problem. They can never expect people to know what those needs might be. In the classroom, they will have to raise a hand or go in for extra help after school. They must let friends know when they don't understand a joke or a movie reference. With family, they will have to take care of their equipment and let me know when it's not working. With strangers, they will have to decide how much they want to tell about their unique hearing device. Even with all these precautions, they may still suffer circumstances in isolation. As the only one with a cochlear implant, they will have to be assertive, confident and ironically—articulate about their needs.

Key Points to Consider

1. Find others in your situation and create a network of support.

2. Help to ensure your child's inclusion at school.

3. Address the challenges of mainstreaming with your child.

12

My First Year Journal: Knowing What to Say

One year nine months old.

Nine months with the implant.

My child has been listening with cochlear implant technology for nine months. In that time, he has learned to say more than 30 words and I am so proud of this accomplishment. He has come far since the time before his surgery when he couldn't hear at all. Language is now a significant part of his life. I had no idea how quickly he would be able to remember new words and their meanings. No one could predict how he would do with the implant. I am convinced we have made the right choice for our child and our family. I believe he will learn to listen and speak and we can support him along the way. He hears well with the cochlear implant and the language center in his brain responds naturally to what he hears. Not only does he acquire vocabulary by remembering what words mean and how to pronounce them, he also is recognizing when to say them. He now practices using words in a specific situation to see how people react. Circumstances dictate his language. Instead of creating scenarios, I encourage him to pay closer attention to his natural surroundings and learn how words are used in a specific context. It will prove that he has truly mastered our language.

Selecting the right word in a situation is a challenge for my child. I know how difficult it can be to use words correctly from my own experience learning German. When we lived in Austria, I wanted to speak like a local but this required an additional study of how ideas are expressed. A slip-up in word choice could mean the difference between a funny comment and an offensive remark. Luckily, my mistakes were taken lightly as I was a foreigner. Never without a "teacher", my Austrian friends were not shy about rectifying any misuse of their language.

At the University, I had been able to study the language further as part of my doctoral research, which required me to translate passages from Austrian/German text into English. In my work, I worried less about grasping the direct translation of each word in a passage and concentrated on capturing the essence of a quote. After studying the context of a paragraph and attempting to fashion a working translation, I always checked with a local to make sure I hadn't inadvertently misused the meaning of a word. On many occasions, I learned new uses of words or how a meaning might change in context or be defined by historical trends in language. Later, we moved to Germany and once again I had to refine my use of words according to another culture. From these experiences, I understand how my child must learn to select the best word to say what he needs to.

At present, my child's language is also becoming more precise as he refines his word categories. From general to specific, he makes an effort to be clear when he communicates. He tries out words in different situations to see how people react. For instance, he seems to know the meaning of the word, "baby" but the term has many uses. I imagine all the questions he might be grappling with in his head. Why does "baby" refer to him when it also means a tiny newborn? Does a "baby" have no hair because many babies do? Is a small animal a "baby" or is it better to say kitten, calf and puppy than baby cat, baby cow and baby dog? Why when I have a tantrum am I acting like a "baby" who makes mommy angry? Why does she smile at me and say I'm her little "baby"?

A single word can be quite illusive in its meaning. I notice this most vividly when my child uses a word out of context and the results are humorous. During dinner out at the local Indian restaurant, my child points to a boy older than himself and declares in an authoritative tone, "Baby!" His comment is taken offensively as the boy looks to his parents complaining, "I'm NOT a baby!" My child stares at him confused by the affront. Just when he had gained enough confidence to use one of his favorite words, context became important and his misuse of the word became an insight into the complexities of our language.

My child's first word was "mama" but I'm not convinced he knew what he was saying. Testing out the familiar consonant vowel combination at the breakfast table in Lexington, Kentucky with his aunt and cousins, he clearly said one of the most beautiful words in the English language and got quite an ovation from the crowd. Soon after, he called my husband "papa" but then turned to me and said "papa". This could only mean he wasn't quite sure what the word meant and was just trying it out.

In books and videos, he had seen an adult character playing with a child, feeding a child, and tucking a child in bed at night. He must have learned a person who could do all those things was called a "papa" and he was satisfied with that word. How could he know there is a difference between mother and father? Aren't they like trucks- more alike then different? What makes a momma distinctive? As I held him in my arms, I reminded my child I was his "momma". I couldn't wait to hear him call me "momma" because it symbolized my special role in his life. Sure enough, one morning he looked into my eyes and clearly said, "Momma". I knew he understood the word was meant just for me. I felt euphoric. His language is becoming more specific.

My child's confidence in his speech is growing and so is his *pronunciation of words. No longer do I have to guess what he is saying through clues in the environment. No longer do I wait for his point to show me what he wants. His voice is clear and consistent. My journal contains a list of eleven words he can clearly pronounce. I have started a second list of words I know he is trying to say but cannot pronounce clearly.*

I believe the muscles in his mouth are becoming stronger when I introduce different types of foods into his diet: pasta, meat (especially chicken), bread with peanut butter, bagel and cream cheese, slices of cheese, banana, milk, water, soup, apples and grapes. After a long day of hard play, he eagerly evaluates the different tastes and textures I place before him at the dinner table. Sampling each one, he chews with tiny baby teeth and learns to control his swallowing although burps sometime escape when air and food mix on their way to the stomach. Good articulation is evidence that my child's cochlear implant is working. He not only hears how words are pronounced but also reproduces them clearly when he speaks.

My child is now one year nine months old and he's quickly becoming a rambunctious toddler. His personality shines through his actions regardless of his cochlear implant. I know he manages his hearing loss in a manner fashioned by his personality: thoughtfully, enthusiastically and creatively. Even though I am very consumed with helping him learn language and maintain his hearing equipment, he stays focused on his own goals: drinking by himself, catching a ball and using a spoon.

I am relieved to observe he is not hindered by his cochlear implant at all, appearing to thrive despite its constant presence in his life. His curiosity abounds and I watch him enjoy pushing boundaries and acquiring new skills. So far, these traits have made it easy for me to teach him how to say new words, such as "marble", "apple" and "hat". He listens and watches us attentively when we talk. He enjoys taking us by the hand around the house, striding with more confidence, gaining strength from practice and our support. Likewise, we continue to follow his lead, teaching him words as he indicates the need for them.

Once my child has learned to pronounce a word with self-confidence, he easily learns rhyming words. By replacing a single letter, he quickly expands his vocabulary. As soon as he is able to say, "moon" we work on "spoon" and then "boom". I follow up by teaching him their meanings. I rely upon children's books following a rhyming format, such as Dr. Seuss', "Green Eggs and Ham" to give him a sample of how rhymes are used in our language. After reading the stories again and again, I pause to see if my child will fill in the rhyming word. Even if he doesn't know the meaning of all the words, he enjoys participating in our reading time together.

My child has begun to say "owie" to let me know he is injured. Touching the stove, he learns a life lesson with a bright red mark on his finger to prove it. Not only aware of his own pain, he also notices when others are hurt. He points to a cut, bug bite or bruise on my leg and says "owie", showing the first signs of empathy. The word gives him the ability to tell me, "I know your hurt mommy because I know what hurt looks like." He understands how it feels to get injured, being an active, athletic boy. His day is spent pushing the limits of his body, practicing balancing and building coordination. He comes from a family of active people and has watched us play sports and exercise. He loves to be pushed in his carriage by his father on long runs through the woods.

My child is now conscious of getting hurt or feeling pain and he has a strong desire to express this emotion to me with a word. When his finger gets pinched at the park; when he bumps his head on a table's edge; when he lands on a knee misjudging the stair height, he says, "owie". Luckily, he learns from his mistakes, making better choices the next time, protecting his body from injury. He has reserved the word "owie" to signal the experience of pain. In tracking his new words with my journal, I can see patterns in his language development to help him learn when to say what.

My child delights in saying, "bye bye". He is learning not only what goodbye means but also when he should say it: at the end of a visit, play date, or party. Some of his favorite words are sparked by an action. He knows "bye" means someone is leaving. He watches them stand up, put their coat on and head for the door. He has also learned to say "bye" as he leaves. As his father swoops down and lifts him to eye level with other adults, he exclaims an enthusiastic "bye bye" and gives a little wave. He knows we will soon head to the car and be on our way home. He will also say "bye" in a store when we go out, making the shopkeepers smile. He will say it to dogs, who are led by their masters away from the park, to cars pulling away and when his favorite video is over. His "bye bye" is a wonderful way to learn how language is bound to situation and he is learning the foundation of social graces. Drawing from his word bank, my child is becoming more skilled at finding the most suitable thing to say in a given situation.

13

Facing Social Challenges

Even if my children's cochlear implant parts are in working order, I know they sometimes struggle to hear. I acknowledge the critical role of our audiologist in helping them adjust the speech processor's programs to address their individual preferences. One month after my son's surgery, we sat patiently in the University of Frankfurt Hospital waiting room to have his implant "activated" and begin programming the speech processor. To our astonishment, an American audiologist ushered us into the testing room. Married to a German, she had been living in Frankfurt for years. What good fortune to be assigned an American who had extensive experience working with cochlear implant patients as the technology became increasingly advanced!

I am always thankful for the people who enter my life at just the right moment, providing extra strength and courage during difficult times. Our first audiologist became a trusted ally and mentor through my son's initial transition into the hearing world. She seemed to take special interest in him as if he was more than just another patient. I think she sensed how alone we were in our journey, living abroad without the support of immediate family. During our appointments, she spent long periods of time carefully programming each electrode individually, a task no longer needed today with improved software. She would listen to me talk about what I was experiencing at home and answer my unending list of questions. Naturally, she was the first person to warn me how louder environments would present a challenge for my son. Parents, seek out an audiologist whom you trust because the cochlear implant's performance depends upon your child's individualize program for the speech processor.

The social cost of noisy places. The social consequences of not hearing well in noisy places can be devastating. In a great sea of people, my children may end up feeling very alone if they are unable to speak with anyone. Groups give them little security as they might for others. Voices intermixing and overlapping cause my children to lose their ability to follow a conversation, preventing them from joining in. I discuss this quandary with my audiologist. Although my children score extremely well on a thorough battery of hearing tests, they are taken inside a sound booth where all variables are controlled.

We continue to tweak the program of their speech processors and are thankful they hear exceptionally well considering the magnitude of their hearing loss. In quiet environments, they listen with ease and can localize where a sound comes from without much trouble. Unfortunately, real life is rarely as tranquil as a sound booth. When we are together in loud environments, I watch my children make a huge effort to single out one voice among many. In restaurants, at parties, and on the playground, background noise becomes especially hard for them to overcome. The effort to participate in conversations often preoccupies them.

I am confident my children hear but it's difficult to know exactly how well they hear at school. Many of my children's teachers assume the cochlear implant corrects hearing loss, presuming they hear the same as other students who listen and speak with great skill. I read in my son's progress reports how he participates fully in group discussions, answering many questions during class. He is eager to share his ideas and confident in his knowledge. However, I wonder if it's tiring to listen intensely for long periods with a cochlear implant.

During an extensive school day, my children must navigate many different learning scenarios: group work in the classroom, gossip with friends at lunch, announcements at the school assembly, directions in PE, communications over the loudspeaker, games in Spanish class, songs in Music class, whispers in the locker bay and hallways, and last minute plans with friends at pick up. Just like me, they may lose focus while they are supposed to be listening especially when they are tired of paying attention. This does not excuse them from trying, but it pays to remind others that although it seems like my children hear extremely well, we can't define exactly what that means.

Social time at school. School is a place where the best social experiences present a hearing challenge for my children, as the acoustics are often abysmal. When my son reaches kindergarten age, we evaluate the acoustics of many classrooms, listening for rumbling air conditioners, squeaky floor surfaces, hissing florescent lights and humming computers as we tour different school buildings. Slick surfaces, bare windows, Smart boards and smooth desktops all encourage sound to grow louder. I point these issues out to teachers who complain of strained voices, struggling against environmental factors to keep students focused and noise levels down.

Lunchtime, recess, group work, assemblies, hallways, and PE all have higher levels of background noise. These situations not only involve a large number of students but also are held in large rooms and open spaces where sound doesn't travel well. Many schools have multipurpose rooms where children interact more freely, but noise in such areas reaches unimaginable proportions. I am amazed at the level of sound children have to put up with in their learning environments, making concentration and socialization difficult. On more than one occasion, my husband and I argue to school administrators that improving the acoustical conditions of classrooms will benefit all children, not just those with hearing loss.

My children respond when they cannot hear. Instinctively, they lean in so their microphones are closer to the person speaking, as you would naturally cup your ear to hear when someone whispers. I have always encouraged my children to advocate for themselves if they cannot hear. Of course, I will do what I can to help them when we are together, acting on their best behalf, leading teacher in-services and fighting for better acoustics. Sometimes, I help facilitate conversations with other children, drawing them in. However, I want them to get help the moment they need it and to let people know when they are having trouble hearing.

Our goal is to make sure they are able to navigate independently in the world; which is the main reason we chose the cochlear implant as treatment for our children's hearing loss. They should never assume others know they cannot hear without their equipment. No one can tell how well my children hear in all environments and situations. They must make their needs clear. They must raise their hands and ask for clarification on instructions in class or when the teacher is providing critical information. With friends, they are less likely to interrupt. They don't want to break the natural flow of conversation. They will begin to lip read and use whatever reasoning power they have to fill in the missing pieces. They know that not every word is critical so they constantly evaluate what is important information and what can be disregarded.

<u>When others don't help.</u> What are the social consequences of not participating in conversations? Attending a school field trip to the local zoo, I notice my son having trouble hearing his friends seated across from him at a picnic table outside. Even though he is close to the others, he has a difficult time keeping up with their jokes and insinuations. The children don't notice his frustration as they are used to interacting with him in the quiet classroom where his ability to follow the teacher's lessons is similar to their own. They cannot understand having to treat him differently depending on the circumstance.

Miscommunication can certainly lead to frustration and isolation. For instance, when someone greets my children with a friendly, "hi!" excessive background noise may prevent them from hearing and their lack of response may hurt the other child's feelings. I have reminded my children to look around carefully when walking past other children. They may not greet them again if they do not reply. Over time, some children stop reaching out if their efforts aren't reciprocated. My children have to fight their natural tendency to avoid eye contact and initiate a greeting.

Even when teachers exhibit empathy towards my children, they may not always understand when it is difficult for them to hear. My children perform well academically and their instructors always remark how difficult it is to believe they were born with such a serious hearing loss. Teachers are generally very impressed with cochlear implant technology and my children's ability to do well in a mainstream classroom. However, if they do not follow directions during a lesson, how much more likely is it for the teacher to accuse them of not paying attention then to check if they actually heard? Once, a frustrated mainstream teacher reprimanded my son by shouting, "You're not listening!" The irony of that statement is significant – at what point does a child with hearing loss stop listening because they can't hear well? When I ask my son about this problem, he insists he has to focus more than his peers in order to keep up with them during the school day. I am proud of his efforts to perform well without assistance.

Challenging acoustical circumstances are often beyond control. On a field trip to the ocean for science class, students were asked to come up in groups to inspect items dredged from the bottom. When my son moved to the table at the incorrect time, both classmates and teachers reprimanded him. His peers assumed he was just eager to see what had been uncovered, ignoring the teacher's instructions. As a chaperone observing the entire event, I know the roar of the boat prevented him from hearing the directions and the error was unintentional.

Unfortunately, teachers are expected to know the difference between a child who is not listening and one who cannot hear. In the classroom, teachers always seat my children in the front row to optimize their hearing but this also has social consequences. As children move into different positions around the room, they interact more naturally with their neighbors and form new friendships. My children feel it is embarrassing to be singled out and treated differently from other children.

My children prefer one-on-one conversations in quiet environments, where they are better able to engage with a friend. My son is full of ideas and the desire to share them. He has the vocabulary and confidence to express his thoughts but prefers a quiet place to do so. My daughter craves individual interaction with friends, giving her implant the best possible circumstances for optimal hearing. But most social settings involve rooms full of people and high levels of background noise, making it a challenge for her to listen and participate.

To help with the noise issues in the classroom, we purchased a sound field FM system for the school. The system amplifies a teacher's voice through a microphone she wears while instructing. Projected by a speaker in the classroom, a teacher should be heard clearly above the background noise. Some teachers falsely believe the FM isn't necessary because their voices are naturally loud. What they don't understand is louder sound isn't always better. Unfortunately, the FM only improves my children's hearing if it is used consistently and correctly. Without training from our audiologist who is located two hours away, teachers are left guessing as to how they should best help my children hear in the classroom. They cannot rely solely on an FM system or just try to keep students quiet. My children must self-advocate with confidence when they are unable to hear.

Key Points to Consider

1. Realize that noisy places have a social cost for your child.

2. Poor acoustics in many school spaces make it difficult to listen and participate.

3. Don't expect others to always understand the needs of your child.

14

My First Year Journal: Action Words

One year ten months old.

Ten months with the implant.

I observe my child suddenly joining nouns and verbs together, giving him the ability to be more specific when he speaks. He is transitioning from infant to young child physically, emotionally and socially. No longer helpless and fragile, my child is a moving bundle of energy. A lively initiator of his own destiny, he often places himself in harm's way by running into the street or grabbing things off the kitchen counter.

I am grateful for the cochlear implant as it makes him better aware of his environment and its potential dangers. I can see the difference without his CI when he is oblivious to the spice jars crashing down from the shelf with a terrible noise, narrowly missing his head. Too busy to heed my many warnings, he at least begins to describe what he observes with a noun verb combination. If he doesn't know a word he makes one up, shouting, "Boom down!" at the spice jars scattering across the floor. Using nouns verb combinations, he can express many ideas for they are the building blocks of English grammar.

This development in my child's speech may be inspired by his fascination with things we do to wield power over our lives. He wants to be the master of his world. Exerting willpower upon his body, his toys, his bath water, and his mom is heady stuff to a young child. The purpose of our activities and their results are most interesting to him, driving the "cause and effect" relationship. My child is quick to notice how I control a situation through my will and he imitates my actions. I can see his bright eyes studying me, thoughts racing, "What are you doing mommy? What's going to happen next? I want to do that!"

Our busy days are filled with activity and verbs describe those actions. He watches me cook, paint pictures, drive the car, search for lost items, and organize our home. I see him pretending to do all of these activities and I encourage him with tiny mixing spoons, paintbrush, and toy steering wheel complete with gearshift. He shadows me wherever I go, mirroring my movements, learning how to do things. I teach him verbs describing my actions as I work: mommy eats, mommy drinks, mommy calls, mommy irons, and mommy jogs. For everything Mommy does, there is a word to describe my action.

My child's first favorite noun/verb pairing comes from an initial taste of power over fragile things. While chasing down a bubble in the backyard, he exclaims, "Bubble pop!" bursting it with full force. I can tell he enjoys the feeling of omnipotence. Saying the words aloud as he pops the bubble reaffirms their meaning and asserts he is acting out his intentions. Soap dripping from his finger; he looks back at me with pride. The bubble is indeed popped. The noun "bubble" describes only what we are making, blowing a thin layer of soap thorough a small circular wand. He is not satisfied anymore by the single naming of a noun.

The wind picks up the airy spheres of liquid, lifting them into the sky, swirling higher and higher. My child watches them rise, prompting me to blow more bubbles. I pass him the wand but he refuses, opting rather to chase after the sparkling balls of light and pop them as they drop within his reach. The excitement of hitting the target is punctuated by his words, "bubble pop". I am confident the cochlear implant enables him to learn language naturally, through observation and imitation, stringing nouns and verbs together.

In the afternoons, our pitched driveway is always a source of creative play. After kicking the ball uphill, my child discovers it always rolls back down to his feet. A favorite game for sunny afternoons, he sends the soccer ball upwards over and over. I become tired just watching him knowing his energy levels far exceed mine. Unexpectedly one day, he shouts with full verve, "Ball up!" before giving it a big kick, shooting the sphere against gravity's pull to the top of the hill. He is aware of what he intends to do and he knows he has the power to do it. He is learning that "ball" and "up" as individual words are not enough to communicate his thoughts. Together they show purpose and this helps him express a specific idea. Saying the words aloud let me know what his intentions are before anything happens. He calls my attention to what he is about to do, trying to impress me with his athletic skill and physical strength.

I give my child examples of noun/verb pairings such as, "Make the blocks fall!" or "Did your milk spill?" I know he needs me to teach him new noun verb combinations as much as possible. I take my responsibility seriously, continuing to engage him throughout the day. I listen carefully for new words he's trying to say so I can help him learn faster. I add different words to the ones he's already saying clearly. I keep my language simple but push him further with unfamiliar vocabulary and new word combinations. For instance, "down" is now a favorite word of his. Wielding toddler power, he gives me directions with a bossy tone when saying, "Down!" He wants his book from the high shelf or to be carried downstairs. Needing to get down, seeing something drop down, or tumbling down, he learns how gravity works.

Down is such an important part of his daily experience he

relates very easily to the outcome. He knows how it feels to go down. Experience teaches him sound can punctuate "down" when a glass falls producing a shattering noise or when tiny Legos spill showering the hardwood floor with pitter pater. When something goes "down" unexpectedly, I see his face processing what happened for a moment before grasping the cause and effect. The incident may produce a cry, a gasp, or the word "down" muttered in a despondent tone.

I decide my child needs to learn the names of basic geometric shapes so we play with them in a multitude of ways. I show him simple shapes of all sizes and colors. I draw circles for him in blue and red so he can trace the line with his finger. I cut triangles out of paper and he peers through the space that remains, the hole of air, trying to understand how he sees a shape that isn't there. We create squares with cereal, pretzels and blueberries eating them afterwards. Offering him a bag of shapes, I ask him to sort them into piles. He carefully examines each one, studying their form, recognizing the pattern.

I explain how shapes are all around him. I show him how the sun is round and a pillow can be square. I ask him to look for the triangular shape in a pine tree and the rectangular shape of a door. He feels the pointed corners of the table and learns how a square's edges connect, attaching a name to the shape of things. We find circles everywhere on our walks together: tires on the bus, bright moon in the night sky, eyes twinkling and round coins in my wallet. Taking the newly issued Euro currency from my hand, he inspects both sides, rolling the edges along his palm. He understands what curved is and how curves form the shape of a circle. Now he says, "circle" to tell me what shape he sees in the picture book. I smile to assure him he has found the right word. We trace circles around a cup onto sheets of paper and then I fill them in drawing animals, flowers and cookies. I teach my child to draw his own simple geometric shapes and begin to write out the word for each, showing him the sacred symbols of our precious language.

Even with new developments in his speech, such as combining nouns and verbs together, my child still sometimes uses sounds or gestures to represent a word. For example, he continues to say "sh-sh-shshshshsh" for water. A sign of his fascination with its physical properties, he attempts to make water sounds. Creating his own "word" for water, he listens carefully producing the sound he hears. Water can be noisy, pounding on the glass panes of our windows and spraying from a slender garden hose. I consider what words I should teach him for these situations. The water "runs" from the faucet but that's quite a stretch for his young mind. Running is something one does with legs, stretching forward towards the empty seat of a park swing. In our language, water runs, pours, spurts, drips, splashes and flows. When will he be ready to know the difference? I know he will learn a new word when he feels motivated and not before.

I often wonder how my child hears the world differently with his cochlear implant. Does water sound the same to him as it does to me? How is it possible to experience music and voice the same as I do? After all, my child's brain is processing mechanically stimulated sound. Wouldn't speech and music heard artificially be in some way unnatural? Implant manufacturers are working on creating programs for the speech processor to specifically enhance the perception of music. Given this move towards refining the programming and user experience, I study my child's ability to articulate speech, song and the overall enjoyment of sound. I watch his reaction not only to music but also to bird song, waves rolling to shore, wind in the trees and other pleasant sounds.

After some thought, I make two important conclusions. First, my child has no memory of sound. Everything heard through the cochlear implant is first hand experience and so his enjoyment is defined more by personal aptitude than by mechanical ability, just like those who hear naturally. Some people take more pleasure in music than others. Some are able to carry a tune better and some can distinguish a birdcall more quickly. Second, I believe my child reproduces a sound to the best of his ability and does so exceedingly well. If he hears the world with a device that alters sound into abrupt unnatural fragments, I would think his speech would also be mechanical sounding, but it is not. When I explain how my child actually hears to friends and strangers alike, I acknowledge the extraordinary nature of the mind and its *ability to make use of artificially produced hearing. Drawing our full attention, my child understands the real power of words. He chooses them carefully, joining noun to verb. I take note; the increasing complexity of his language is good material for my journal.*

15

Understanding Family Dynamics

During hours and hours of close proximity, my children observe us carefully to create a "family" category in their mind- - one they fit into. I imagine my son asking himself, "How am I like these people who are my family and how am I different?" Besides "Papa and I like to play ball" and "Mama and I like to build", a comparison of physical features makes the list. After checking the hallway mirror, he confirms: blue eyes, sandy hair, freckles and peach colored skin all the same as mom. Tall build, bright eyes and big smile from dad. Having thoroughly investigated his own speech processor, microphone and cable, he discovers mom and dad don't wear those items to hear.

Recognizing familial differences is disconcerting to my children. I could tell even simple variations of blue eyes made my daughter wonder, do we belong together? I am your child. Why are we not exactly alike? Although most concerns of this kind eventually faded, their persistence regarding one particular topic continued, "Why can't I hear when you and daddy can?" It's a tough question to answer as we operate on the premise everyone in our family can hear, although my children do so with their cochlear implants and we through our ears. Yet, there are visual and physical differences in how my children hear. This variation in our family eventually has to be acknowledged.

Explaining hearing loss. When my son is ready to learn why his ears are built differently from ours, I prepare a brief response. I keep my answer simple for his young mind. I tell him everyone has many copies of a tiny "book" inside their body called DNA. It tells how a person is supposed to turn out from the moment their heart begins beating- not only hair color or texture but also how ears are built. The body follows the instructions in its book to develop from infancy through childhood into adulthood, eventually creating the person we are destined to become. He listens carefully as I explain how my family wrote some things found in his book and others were written by his father's-- features from mama and height from papa. Combined they make him a unique, beautiful child.

In regards to hearing, I tell him papa and I were born with ears that are different from his according to our books, which were written by his grandparents. Since his father and I wrote his DNA book together, I explain how the combined effect might generate unusual traits from both families' heritage. In other words, everyone has a predetermined set of features according to their families, which create a singular being. The body we are given by our parents makes life easier or more challenging for us, depending on what we hope to accomplish in our lifetime.

Once he is older and ready for more information, I tell him scientists like to study how our DNA "book" works. They want to understand more about the complicated "language" it is written in. If scientists can read a person's DNA book, doctors can sometimes help them. According to the instructions in my book, I explain, my inner ears have tiny hairs that shake against a road where messages are sent to the brain when I listen to sound. The hairs in his ears, I clarify, are missing because of the way his DNA book is written, so the cochlear implant does the messenger work instead. Whatever way you choose to explain it, a child should understand the basic causes of his or her hearing loss and how the body works.

Much later, I am surprised to learn my son had interrupted his third grade Science lesson on the senses with the comment, "That's not how I hear!" Proceeding to the front of the room, he gave an impromptu mini-lecture to his fellow classmates on the cochlear implant. I am impressed by his courage and comfort with the subject. I am also glad we had discussed the topic when it first arose. Ultimately, I know my children have an identity apart from their hearing loss. As they grow, their personality, interests and talents will overshadow the technology they use to hear, letting their true identity shine through.

<u>Recognizing different experiences.</u> My nuclear family has remarkable balance. We are two females and two males, two hearing and two with hearing loss. My children were born on the same day two years apart and have the same bilateral sensorineural hearing loss. Our family is defined by similarities and differences created by the predictable yet random laws of nature; each of us a unique but required puzzle piece in the clan portrait. Before my daughter was born, I felt outweighed by male dominated activity, with its teasing and tough it out approach to life. Female friendships are based on intimate conversations, shared secrets and bonding through dialogue. Said to have more advanced maturity, leading to complex use of vocabulary, girls are expected to have superior language skills.

I wonder, how does a girl with hearing loss struggle if social interaction with peers is so important? Girls are said to use many more words in the day than boys. How will hearing loss impede my daughter's ability to learn the latest inside joke, pop song or texting shorthand? Will her cochlear implant enable her to follow the quick pace of her female peers? Unfortunately, bullying may be more verbal in girls. How well will my daughter be able to respond to a verbal attack if it arises? Will she have the words to confront her aggressors?

Boys, on the other hand, might naturally talk less, acting out their impulses or passions by building or competing at games.

Certainly, I have found people to be more forgiving of weak conversational skills in boys. Unusual or unfitting statements may be disregarded more easily coming from my son than my daughter. It is no surprise boys will spend time discussing their favorite team scores, video game strategies or burping techniques. Male bullying might involve pushing or punching. Is a boy's cochlear implant equipment more a hindrance than his language skills when physical-based activities are expected of male interaction? We have decided our son will not play full contact sports such as lacrosse to protect his cochlear implant. An unanticipated consequence of limited participation in sports is its effect on social groups. Fortunately, my children have found their place on the tennis court. The general nature of male and female interaction may impact my children, but our family's stability remains their most important refuge in difficult times.

I constantly work to help maintain the balance in my family, a balance challenged by hearing loss. Making slight adjustments when needed, I act as a buffer, interpreter and problem solver when I can. If possible, I turn awkward situations into positive ones. At a recent voice lesson, my daughter was instructed to cup her ears with her hands during a long run of vocal scales. Using techniques professional singers might incorporate into their practices for directing sound into the ears; students become much more self aware of their voices. After a dutiful minute of holding her hands around ears unable to hear any pitch, I whisper to her teacher, "She can't hear through her ears." The challenge is to avoid discouragement during regular family activities. In a burst of inspiration, the voice teacher raised my daughter's hand to cup her microphone, asking her to sing the scales again. To our amazement, she sang every pitch on key. Her teacher and I begin to conceive a microphone for cochlear implants with a small raised edge to help catch sounds and channel them inside the same way our ears do. At that moment, my daughter's differences were lessened slightly through creative problem solving and a determined mindset unwilling to back down from a challenge.

My daughter asks me if I know what it is like not to hear.

Late at night, she prepares herself for sleep. While detaching her fanny pack and handing me her cochlear implant equipment, she realizes how her "ear" is different from mine. I am able to hear during the night. This disparity directly affects not just her life experiences but ours as well. Keenly self-aware, she is ready to share her side of the story, helping me understand the world from her perspective. She describes her silent time at night like being in a room all by oneself-- quiet, with no interruptions.

I tell her as I fall asleep, I still hear things: the gentle breathing of her sleeping father, cats prowling the house and rain pounding on the roof. When fast asleep, I have no memories of sound outside my dreams. Mother's instinct still sharp, I do listen for cries in the night or restless feet on the hallway floor. I tell her I wake for many noises: a harp playing on my phone's alarm or voices from the TV murmuring in the next room.

In those minutes of calm before sleep, my child continues her stream of thoughts without hearing, sharing a few last stories of the day. In the dark, she whispers clearly. She manipulates her voice by controlling her breath and does not stop talking just because she cannot hear. In my imagination, I face her underwater in the pool, her mouth moving and me unable to hear her. She reads my lips easily understanding my speech. There is no avoiding the fact; we are different.

Family harmony. Family dynamics either build harmony at home or erode it. Each person in my family adds his or her own unique perspective to a situation. Differences create tension in family life and hearing loss is a significant deviation in ours. Like any group, constructed by shades of difference, we must find a form of unity that works for all. As we face challenges, we must be unified. We must choose to stand side-by-side through all types of life experiences. More often than not, we are conscious of the changes in our lives due to the constant presence of hearing loss. But like most families, a deep bond forms during times spent together, on vacation as well as at the audiologist. Individual pursuits are balanced with what's best for everyone and sometimes hearing loss needs to be a priority.

My children are fighters, even though they don't realize it

because they must constantly work to get enough information from their surroundings or risk falling behind. My job is to assist them if I can, ease their challenges, and help others be more sensitive to their needs. I learn over time how to be an effective but subtle advocate, sometimes smoothing out a challenge before they ever get wind of it. During the first years of my son's life, I push aside the thought, "Why did this happen?" instead focusing on "What can I do about it?" I knew I would have to adapt, stretching my character to embrace our new circumstances. Deep down, I want to continue living according to our own rules, as we have always done. I do not want to change who I am and what kind of mother I am. At some point differences have to be faced and a common ground found to keep the balance.

Key Points to Consider

1. Think about how you will explain the cause of hearing loss to your child.

2. Reflect on how personality and gender might influence the development of your child's language.

3. Encourage family members to play a positive role in your child progress.

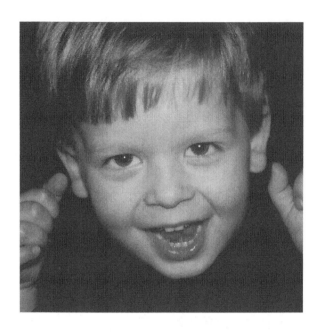

16

My First Year Journal: Needing More Words

One year eleven months old.

Eleven months with the implant.

My child continually seeks out situations he knows will help him learn new words. I give him more wiggle room to assert his interests, hoping to find out what motivates him. Moving freely around our home, led by his curiosity, I watch him take particular interest in activities where language is central. He lets me know what types of sources he wants to learn from: books, television, or with me during playtime. He craves new words now like he needs a healthy breakfast in the morning. He wants to understand what I am saying and to be an active participant in the conversation. Except for evenings and weekends with his father and our regular playgroup, he is primarily with me. I know I need to build variety into his learning experience, for his sanity and mine. Discovering new words is an essential part of his day. He gathers them like tiny pebbles along the path to the playground. Where can he find the words he needs?

My child is drawn to children's videos with content containing reading concepts. When I was young, Sesame Street introduced primary phonetics to me on the television, with Cookie Monster and Big Bird as my teachers. Making learning fun with visually bright and animated characters, children's television shows draw in my child. Repeating "the word of the day" or a sound as it's found in many words helps me continue introducing age appropriate concepts to my child. We have many more programs to choose from than in the days of my youth. Rather than using television as a baby sitter, I watch shows together with my child and try to explain things that appear in the scenes or reemphasize new words as they are introduced.

My child prefers T.V. programs introducing new vocabulary with comedy. Mesmerized by the funny antics created just for children his age, he's barely aware he is learning language. Captivated by the humor, he anticipates the characters catch phrases or laughs at their silly use of words. I have found humor is a great way to engage my child. It is a form of language bringing joy to our lives and happiness to our hearts. We laugh at a monster, who can never get enough cookies. My child's insatiable sweet tooth and constant plea for cookies are not much different. Humor requires him to listen carefully. He not only understands what is being said but also why it is funny. I am so grateful to know my child will be able to appreciate many forms of humor with the cochlear implant.

Sometimes, my child intentionally does the opposite of what I say. As the sky darkens outside, I tell him, "We are all done. Put the toys away. It's time to clean up." He might give me a sly grin and dump the box of Legos on the floor. Not only does he understand the meaning of the words "done" and "clean up", he also knows he does not want to stop playing. Instead of telling me so, he uses actions to communicate exactly how he feels. Although I am irked by his reaction, I have to admit I am impressed with his quick response to my language. Collecting the tiny colored blocks from the floor, I

97

give him a sympathetic smile and say, "I know, I don't want to stop playing either."

Often, he understands what I'm telling him enough to do just the opposite. If I tell him, "Come over here, it's time to go." He may only pick up the word "go" and take off in another direction, avoiding my stern face and the warning tone in my voice. I know he must use his knowledge of language to make a judgment call when to obey and when to resist. One afternoon, I find him hiding under the clothing racks of our favorite department store, ignoring my desperate calls like many children his age. Even though his mischievousness can be wearing, as any parent can tell you, my child is taking his first steps towards independence, proving his knowledge of language has grown.

While searching through the latest releases, I intentionally avoid television programs featuring characters like "Elmo" or the "Teletubbies" whose shrill voices and unconventional language are difficult for my child to understand. I need to make it easy for him to hear and I am always trying to reduce extraneous noises if possible. Even though he enjoys watching T.V., I do not have it on in the background when we are doing other activities. Why should he have to work harder to process sound than he already has to, even with his cochlear implant in working order?

Interestingly, many popular T.V. shows for children such as, "Thomas the Train" or "Dora" have characters with foreign accents. I purposely expose my child only to American English, as he improves his pronunciation by imitating what he hears. I am very aware he has to make up for lost time. I record in my journal he now says, "ball" with an "all" sound after months of using the proto word "beh". He needs to hear the correct pronunciation of a word over and over to be confident of his own articulation. Television is especially helpful to my child as he must listen using his cochlear implant to characters in shaggy costumes who don't move their lips.

Even though I enjoy being the primary teacher of my child, I know the value of playgroups as an experience where he can learn new words. The more I give my child opportunities to be with his peers, the more he discovers one can learn from anyone, even a person not quite three feet tall. Sometimes, it is difficult for me to gage exactly how simple or complex my language should be when I speak with my child. I like to tell him how to say something correctly and push him to use more specific vocabulary but all is lost if I loose his attention in the process. The children in his playgroup have a great advantage over me as role models in that they are only ahead of my child's speech and language by varying degrees. They were more recently at his level of vocabulary and articulation.

I notice how older children will inadvertently teach the younger ones new words as they play. Words commonly used by ringleaders in the playgroup make a great impression on my child. Quick to learn, they push themselves in order to compete with their older rivals by using "grown up" words. However, I also notice the language of my son's playmates is often held constant at the lowest common denominator. Even though older children can speak with greater clarity, they sometimes choose simple words and sentences preferring rather to be understood. They seem to want younger children to follow them at all costs.

I can relate, knowing Germans will sometimes speak to me slower and with greater simplicity, assuming I am not able to understand advanced vocabulary. I must concede that other children hold a great value for my child as teachers of language. Amused by his latest attempts to imitate a friend, I think, "Now, where did he pick up that word?" I never underestimate the power of peer pressure and the importance of playgroups in the development of my child's language.

In my journal, I keep track of preferred sources for new words along with vocabulary my child tries to say, even when he mispronounces it. Most recently, I write: truck, pasta, house, egg, bee, pen, man and "choo" for train. The list reminds me to help him practice pronouncing certain words. I know it will take time to learn their meanings thoroughly. I mark those he can say clearly with a star, like the words "egg" and "bee" so I can introduce rhyming words. My child's growing awareness of the world helps him practice language. He will spontaneously say words when seeing something he recognizes in a video or book. Often, he looks over at me and waits for an explanation. This is a "teaching moment" as I know I have his full attention.

Music is another vehicle capturing my child's attention and motivating him to learn language. He listens to many forms of music: theme songs from his favorite television shows, CDs of contemporary music, or lullabies I sing to him before bed. Together, we sing children's songs and he will make up his own tune, banging on the pots and pans from my kitchen. He will spring from the couch and march around the room when the characters on a video are dancing or singing.

Before he could hear, I know he was able to feel music. I remember lying on the wooden floor of our living room in Wiesbaden with my child nearby, less than a year old, looking up at the beautiful moldings of our turn-of-the century apartment with Beethoven's symphony blasting from a nearby speaker. The floor vibrating beneath us, I knew my child's hearing aids would not enable him to hear what I was hearing. I was determined to have him experience music. I moved above him, squeezing his hand to the rhythm, allowing him to see in my eyes what the music made me feel.

With the cochlear implant, my child hears the melody as well as the words of a tune—the poetry of song and it helps him learn language. Knowing he can hear music with his cochlear implant helps us find a direction for his education. As I compare and contrast preschools across the country specializing in language immersion for children with cochlear implants, the Jean Weingarten Peninsula Oral School for the Deaf stands out with its full integration of music into every student's daily experience. Using familiar childhood tunes, such as "The Wheels on the Bus" and "Frere Jacques", teachers sing about themes or school activities to help their students with hearing loss learn in a way that appeals to children. Song is a place where my child always finds new words. His appetite for vocabulary is increasing and his cochlear implant can handle the pace.

Books continue to be a tremendous resource for new words. Outside the German air is chilly. I sip Pfefferminze tea while snuggling with my child under our warm Federbett with his favorite book by Lois Ehlert, "Feathers for Lunch". I know why he picks this book out again and again from his library. Filled with bright graphic pictures of different birds, each is identified by its scientific name. The plot is simple but engaging, a cat on the loose in the garden. He knows the story well, understanding the concept of inside and outside. The cat's bell warns the birds of a predator nearby with a "jingle jingle". I am pregnant with my second child. We have been advised to test her hearing shortly after birth as she has a greater chance of having hearing loss due to her brother's condition. I find a few children's books on welcoming a new baby sister into the family.

17

Breaking Stereotypes

General perceptions about people with hearing loss will change as cochlear implant technology becomes increasingly widespread. Will cochlear implants eventually break stereotypes about the Deaf? I understand the reality of raising children with hearing loss and exactly how cochlear implants have changed the outcome of their lives in a positive way. I know the "unfamiliar" world of hearing loss provokes feelings of anxiety or sympathy and stereotypes about it may have a negative impact on behavior. I won't meet anyone envious or admiring of my children's hearing condition. Assumptions about them will be made; expectations about their abilities adjusted. I have fought these presumptions at every turn.

<u>Assumptions about hearing loss.</u> People are impressed with my children's success as it defies common assumptions about

profound hearing loss. For instance, with their cochlear implants, my children speak with such clarity as to "fool" others into thinking they have hearing. Their reaction to sound is not unlike those of their age and their speech is as articulate as their peers. Yet, they do not hear as others do and this difference makes their achievements all the more astonishing. Their academic success is so unexpected, so unlikely, to many it becomes the standard by which "regular" children should achieve. Turning to their own child, I know parents ask, "If a kid with hearing loss can get all As, then why can't you?" I know my children work extremely hard to maintain high grades and to participate in all activities. Their hearing loss is a barrier they must live with but it won't stop them from trying. I like to think my children's success is not singular, but rather an example of how cochlear implants are changing the outlook for many who have profound hearing loss. If stereotypes about the deaf are outdated, then they hurt the circumstances of children with cochlear implants.

Stereotypes and expectations. I believe in my children's ability to listen and speak, but I know others may not. Once their teachers, friends, and later on employers and colleagues find out they have hearing loss, how will it affect their expectations? At school, when will they be selected as a star in a play, to lead the team on the sport's field, or to represent the class? Later on, when will they be entrusted with key negotiations, presentations, and clients for an employer? How much harder will they have to work to prove what they can do? I hope their hearing loss won't be a factor in their achievements but I have to wonder how it might.

Before my children were born, I never thought much about how other children with profound hearing loss made their way in the world. I knew the story of Helen Keller and had seen Marlee Matlin act in movies. What did these profoundly deaf women and their accomplishments have to do with my children? What impressions have they created by their performances? Their public lives show what people with profound hearing loss can achieve. However, everything they attained and all their success was without cochlear implants. My children learned about Helen Keller during a school

103

assembly. Helen was portrayed as a tragic figure, but one who overcame tremendous obstacles. Sitting cross-legged on the floor of the school auditorium, I wonder if it occurred to my children that they too were born into a silent world. Could they relate to the heroine at all? What did their classmates take away from the story? What did they learn about hearing loss? Did they gain knowledge, empathy, or admiration?

After listening to the presentation, the children left the auditorium with the impression life is difficult with hearing loss, rendering a person quite helpless and isolated. Stereotypes are built on the little information or misinformation people have been exposed to over time. Sadly, the school neglected to inform their students how deaf and blind children live today, leaving Helen's story isolated in time. Her life might be the only impression the children have of deafness. Yet, prospects for kids implanted early in life with bionic technology are higher than ever before. My children should help break stereotypes about persons with profound hearing loss, established by those who came before the cochlear implant was available.

My children have encountered many stereotypes about hearing loss over the years, such as the assumption they know sign language. Most people are cognizant of the visual method for communication the Deaf may use, having seen someone signing on T.V. or perhaps at a children's recital. Present at public performances, sign language interpreters validate the inclusion of those who cannot hear. When someone learns my children have bilateral profound hearing loss at birth, he or she often presumes they understand American Sign Language. Contrary to what many believe, signing is no longer an obligatory skill for children born without hearing.

Having no access to sound until their first birthday, my children's language development was already significantly delayed. For this reason, my husband and I decided against a mixed communication approach or "total communication", which combines speech, sign, and or lip-reading, exposing them only to spoken English. They had to make up for lost time, increasing their level of concentration on listening and speaking. We focused all our efforts on getting them the best speech and language instruction possible and supporting our initiative at home. This direction was in tune with our decision to treat the children's hearing loss with cochlear implants. We believed a visual language would distract from their listening and speaking.

A new identity. By not teaching our children to sign, we also take a dramatic step away from deaf culture and it's identity. Language groups people of a culture together. Living abroad, my English made me an American and Europeans often assumed things about my personal character. My speech prevents me from going incognito with the locals. It also draws me to strangers sitting nearby in a neighborhood coffeehouse, whose familiar words strike me like a stream of light bursting through thick clouds of guttural German. "Where are you from?" I eagerly ask, hoping to strike up a conversation. Having little more in common than a shared language, we soon became acquainted.

If the purpose of a cochlear implant is to provide an adequate range of sound for an infant to learn language, then this must be the priority. By learning to listen and speak early in life, my children are a part of Generation CI (CI refers to Cochlear Implant). However, these children still have profound hearing loss when their microphones are removed. This difference distinguishes them from most people but does not become a hindrance. Once they master English, my children can study American Sign or any other language of their choosing. Twelve years after his cochlear implant gave him access to sound, my son is now deeply entrenched in the study of Latin and is anxious to study German, the language of his heritage and birthplace.

A new stereotype causing confusion for children with profound hearing loss is the assumption that clear speech indicates good hearing. Even though my children's voices can be easily understood, there are circumstances when they are not able to hear well. More than likely, they will not let on to the casual observer. The struggle won't be seen in their faces. Eyes remaining steady and focused, intent on the speaker, they may attempt to play along or disengage entirely, distracted by their own thoughts. This makes it hard for people to grasp how well they are hearing. People assume the cochlear implant totally corrects hearing loss. While it is the best technology yet offered to the profoundly deaf, my children may still not hear as well in loud spaces as their hearing peers.

Resolving health issues by wearing glasses or wearing a cochlear implant is a reasonable comparison to most. Yet, these remedies are very different. A person wearing glasses has corrected vision. So much so, we allow them to drive a car. In conversations, people are often less tolerant with another's inability to hear. Asking to repeat what someone says once too often may elicit the question, "Are you deaf?" Hearing is never constant, even for those who don't rely on cochlear implants. We all cope with different hearing challenges and have to adjust. Yet, rarely do people have patience enough to ensure my child is hearing what needs to be heard.

Another stereotype of children with profound hearing loss is they are less able to learn than their peers. Teachers and school administrators tend to assume my children's hearing will prevent them from performing at or above grade level. Their difference is assumed to have academic consequences. Success in the classroom for those with profound hearing loss is considered the exception not the rule for some teachers.

Even though a child's Individualized Education Program (IEP) is developed to help identify academic goals, a hopeless complacency may permeate the team's outlook. Once, we were told outright at an IEP meeting it was unrealistic to expect our children to catch up with classmates. How could such a judgment be made? Upon entering a private school for which there was no formal IEP and no legal support for special education, my children became regular students, like the rest. Their teachers are aware of their hearing loss but are not required to make concessions. In this type of environment, my responsibility for their academic success grew.

In my effort to understand what academic challenges my children may face, I came upon the assertion that profound hearing loss often prevents people from reading above a fourth grade level. Realizing this could potentially be a reality for my children left me deeply dismayed. In a family like mine, higher education is prioritized above all else. Such a grim academic forecast drives me harder to find ways to help my children. I will not lower my expectations.

I remember how excited I was when my son learned to read. It seemed like a huge milestone, guaranteeing rich communication with all who shared his language without relying on hearing and freeing him from a dependency on the implant. Fully connected to the world through newspapers, novels, poetry and websites, his ability to read is an irrevocable skill. Both my children have a true and passionate love of reading. No doubt, the cochlear implant was a big part of reaching such an achievement. When a child has a high level of reading and academic performance, teachers will not need to provide extra attention to ensure success at school.

As cochlear implants influence life with hearing loss, many questions arise. How independent can children with bionic ears be? Initially, a child's caretakers must provide intensive speech and listening training when language is developing. They must be consistently involved with their child's progress. Are children with cochlear implants ready to make their way through the school experience on their own? The better a child hears, the more independent he can be. School is a good place to practice independent living, a catalyst for changing the course of history, and a new chapter in the chronicles of hearing loss. The current cochlear implant, while alleviating even the most profound hearing loss, is surely not the final answer. Our family and others like ours forge the unexplored trail made possible by the cochlear implant, tough pioneers in an uncharted wilderness, paving the way for future generations like those before us.

Key Points to Consider

1. Your child will defy many stereotypes about deafness.

2. Keep academic and social expectations high for your child.

3. Realize some people won't change their view of hearing loss.

18

My Second Year Journal: Confidence

Two years and two months old.

Fourteen months with the implant.

With growing confidence, my child articulates his needs verbally. I am learning more about him through his preferences: books he favors reading, toys he regularly pulls out for play, and foods he enjoys eating. Words help him communicate these preferences to me. They have bolstered his convictions, making his intentions very clear. As self-awareness increases, he learns how to make himself happy and in doing so his individuality strengthens. Like me, he seems to be very opinionated. Today, he led our playtime together. We read, "Quick as a Cricket" by Audrey Wood and "Planting a Rainbow" by Lois Ehlert, then work the crank of a giant metal top so its colors swirl and blend, followed by a snack of strawberries and mild German "Butterkase" cheese. As sure as the satisfaction on his face, my child's words serve their purpose when he is understood.

Misunderstanding brings confusion and frustration. "No!" he shouts, exasperated when I don't know what he wants. Confidence will help guide his language. Later on, if he can express himself confidently, then it won't matter whether he speaks in front of a lecture hall of colleagues or across the table to a dear friend. He will know how to voice his thoughts with clarity and intent. For now, we work on confident use of his favorite words.

Becoming a big brother defines a new role for my child and as expected, the shock of a sibling inspires a burst of new favorite words. He regularly exclaims, "baby, baby, baby" to his infant sister in a rush of excitement, now having a constant companion to badger and love. Born in Germany on his birthday two years to the day, my daughter's permanent presence in our family is a major source of entertainment for my son. He is fascinated by her every move and regularly gives her cheek a friendly peck. Her radically different temperament forces me to abandon all the skills and experience I had so diligently acquired. She is a beauty with heart shaped face and strong legs that bend and kick with great vigor.

We know her chances for having hearing loss are greater than average. We have to be prepared for either outcome. If she has profound hearing loss, we know what to do. Instead of spending time researching our options, we can just enjoy her and plan for the cochlear implant surgery. If not, we will certainly have less audiology and therapy appointments to schedule. Our decision to have another child comes with plenty of significant unknowns, but all parents take their chances when intertwining the genetic codes of family trees together. We know we will love our second child as much as the first and we excitedly anticipate her birth. Accepting whatever condition she has, we will take full responsibility for our child's life. No amount of testing can change our resolve. During the course of my pregnancy, many people assure us this child would hear. I am less certain but friends and family concur; we can't possibly have two children with hearing loss!

Shortly after the birth of my daughter, a young German

*attendant quietly enters the stark hospital room as I rest to do
a newborn hearing screening. Because my first child has
hearing loss, the doctor requires a test be performed before I
leave for home. While I hold my sleeping child, she gently
pushes the ear buds into place and consults the screen of her
instrument.*

    *Studying the curve of my daughter's tiny eyelashes, I can't
shake a growing feeling of uncertainty as the readings are
recorded. I prepare myself for all scenarios: hearing, not
hearing and anywhere in-between. Yet, something seems
amiss. I look around the sparsely decorated room. The window
is open. Wouldn't we need a quiet environment to get the most
accurate evaluation? She performs the test quickly and
without much interest. I hope she knows what she is doing.
The results have important ramifications for our family. If
only one in a thousand babies is born with profound hearing
loss, then this particular attendant may never discover a child
that can not hear among the newborns. Rather, she will have
seen a significant amount of negative test results. For the
screening to actually be worth the effort and cost to provide it,
I hope the proverbial "needle in the haystack" is found, even if
it is my child.*

    *The doctor came in that evening to inform me my daughter
could hear. After sharing the news with family, I find my
doubts hard to shake. Our doctors had been wrong before
when they insisted my son could hear. I had to be sure the
results were not a false negative. I decide to take my daughter
to our audiologist in Frankfurt to have her reexamined where
we find her ear openings are so small, the ear buds will not
stay in place. An exact seal is required or the test will be
inaccurate. After trying different sizes and a few inventive
tricks to keep them from popping out, our audiologist settles
on multiple screenings to guarantee the validity of her results.
Again, my mother instincts are correct even though the
doctors insist otherwise. My second child also has a profound
hearing loss in both ears. We are once more in the situation of
having the rare condition of rare conditions— two children
with the same degree of hearing loss. How could the newborn
hearing screening, so widely touted as the answer to early
diagnosis, be imprecise? What if I hadn't made the effort to*

drive the 30 minutes to Frankfurt, taking extra time to visit our trusted audiologist? Where would that have left my daughter and her early intervention? I'm not sure if the attendant who tested my daughter at the hospital ever found out that she had not done her job in identifying a solid case of hearing loss, but I have sympathy for any family having to second guess her test results. The corrected diagnosis is difficult to explain to all who share in our surprise.

While we attend to the newly identified hearing loss of our daughter, my son becomes more verbal, self-advocating his needs in the face of sibling competition. What better motivation for learning language than to compete with the angry cries of a newborn! An early riser, he digs through his drawers exclaiming, "Pants!" when only the blue pair with cuffs will do. Later on, we head out to the farmer's market but not before he looks at me with open hands. "Shoes?" he asks. I think back to the days when I first felt confident he could understand the word "shoes". Now, he enunciates it clearly and I don't take any part of that simple evolution for granted. I am suspicious of his interest in these everyday words. Especially when our new baby doesn't wear pants and shoes yet. Could it be he is looking for a way to assert his superiority? He observes her dependence on me and busies himself with the skills needed to get dressed, manipulating buttons and zippers, making knots of his shoelaces.

He begins to say "one" and "two", so I teach him the nursery rhyme "one two, buckle my shoe", singing as we fold the laces into rabbit ears. We begin to count things together and he realizes the value of "one" when there is only one more cookie left in the box or there is time for one more game before bed. After one is gone there is no more. Likewise, two of something can be a pair, belonging together. My son knows he must find two matching brown socks before his shoes go on. Friends who visit us ask him, "How old are you?" He carefully bends his tiny fingers into a peace sign but not without saying the word, "Two!" At two years old, my son wants "more" of everything and can tell me with great conviction. This is his way of letting me know he likes something or he's having fun. My son's need to express himself is so strong that he babbles a lot and uses many words when not wearing his CI. His self-confidence *grows.*

Back in Frankfurt for a programming appointment, my son contributes more actively to his audiology sessions. Instead of a passive patient, to be observed and acted upon, he is now a full participant in the process of adjusting his cochlear implant program to hear better. From his tiny chair in the sound booth where he can only hear beeps or words read over an intercom, he listens carefully and reacts the instant he hears by placing a plastic coin down the narrow slot of a toy game board. He learns quickly how to signal the audiologist and the games make it easy to hold his interest. She tests how well he hears at each decibel level and with every appointment, he improves. A collaborative team effort, our audiologist can make recommended changes to the program of his speech processor based on the best possible use of the cochlear implant technology.

How different this method is from his first audiology appointment, where each electrode was programmed individually like tuning the keys of a piano. Our audiologist looked for physical reactions of discomfort- the blink of an eye or the twitch of a hand, indicating the sound was too loud. She worked very carefully; gradually increasing the amount he could hear so as not to startle him. How much more efficient for my son to take the lead in programming his speech processor, a task we perform once every three months. Even when using the latest software updates, the subjective nature of hearing will always be a factor in programing. Only my son knows how the world sounds through his device.

Significant advances in software improve the ease of programming by the time my daughter is ready to hear with her implant in 2002. Rather than adjust the strength of each electrode in a painfully long series of audiology appointments, a base line program is uploaded as soon as the surgery wound heals. In follow up sessions, maxims are tested and increased. The goal of each update is to give my daughter access to a broad range of sounds as quickly as possible. Our new audiologist in California works in collaboration with my daughter's speech therapist and preschool classroom teacher to ensure the best possible hearing in different types of settlings. At each visit, we are given an audiogram showing my child's response to sound in the testing booth. I track how each change results in better hearing. The scores gradually improve with each adjustment until she can hear all the speech sounds, including the soft high tones of "f", "s" and "th". It gives me great comfort to know exactly what she can hear, even if it is in a sound proof room. This is my second time through the start up phase for a cochlear implant and I also have more self-assurance.

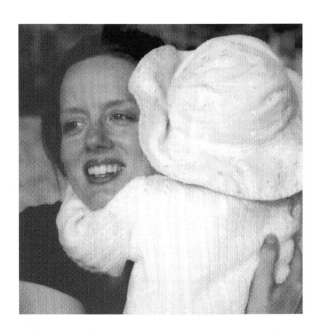

19

Raising Expectations

With a grateful heart, I include my children as part of the first true generation of cochlear implant recipients defined by the significant number of infants implanted with a hearing device for life. As a group, these children will have the ability to pursue their dreams in numbers never before imagined. They will force the world to acknowledge their presence with clear voices and a remarkable ability to listen. Unlike their predecessors-- those with hearing loss who had to overcome tremendous physical and social barriers to achieve their goals, "Generation CI" will follow their dreams by communicating at a higher level to a broader audience with greater ease. The growing number of candidates who can best benefit from the implant will push cochlear implant programs to refine their offerings to meet the needs of infants and very young children.

The biggest challenge for Generation CI is waiting for society to catch up and accept their true potential. In this new reality, no more will a person be perceived as accomplished "despite their hearing loss" or achieve a goal far above expectations. Rather, this legion of children with CIs will reach father and contribute more as a group. Consequently, the world will come to expect a different outcome for the diagnosis of hearing loss.

Hightened expectations. The children of Generation CI will be expected to hear, well enough to manage through spoken language. I know cochlear implant technology is remarkable because I interact with my children as if they hear me. I am confident they do. When I call, they typically come unless they are acting like any child engrossed in a favorite activity. They listen from the back of the car, from the next room at home, from across the tennis court and from the back of the classroom. I do not think about my distance from them when I talk. I do not raise my voice or face them directly when speaking, unless their behavior warrants it. I do not think about their hearing loss when I am with them until there is a breakdown in communication.

For all children with cochlear implants, listening should be as natural as breathing, done without thought. Bionic ears involve no delay in hearing, with sound traveling along the electrode at a remarkable speed. Any assistance the cochlear implant provides in helping ease communication with others is precious for it encourages potential relationships to develop and improves social "survival" skills. The gift of hearing provided by the cochlear implant raises expectations for Generation CI's level of independence. My children may not hear as they should all the time, this I acknowledge, but I am confident they have the skills to get through most circumstances without the help of others— entirely on their own.

Beyond language acquisition, the cochlear implant increases a child's connection with the world in a deep and meaningful way. My children hear not only speech but also all kinds of environmental sounds with their bionic ears. The repetitive roar of the ocean and the quiet coo of a baby add meaning to events in their lives without the constructs of language. They learn from nonverbal sounds, as hearing is a sense organ. With her cochlear implant, my daughter is able to distinguish if a piano scale is "happy" or "sad" by its quality of sound, identifying it as "major" or "minor". She corrects her mistakes when playing piano by "ear", shifting her hands up or down the keys. Nonverbal sounds also enhance the sensations my children experience.

When we eat dinner at a Mexican restaurant, they taste rich refried beans and spicy tomato salsa, take in the brightly colored abstract paintings of Latin landscapes, and smell garlic encrusted fajitas. They also hear oil sizzling on the grill, the crunching of nachos as they bite down and the joyful rhythms of a Mariachi band singing lyrics expressively in Spanish. The evening out results in a multifaceted saturation of cultural expression, including many significant sounds. I no longer underestimate how much "background" noise impacts our state of mind. I have become sensitive to how sound provides us with information, influencing our emotional reaction to the surroundings. The purring of our cat always brings a smile to their faces.

Of course, not all sounds are pleasant. Anger in my voice stops my children in their tracks. At the movies, we all flinch as a car suddenly explodes on screen with a booming "shaabang". My children have learned to pay attention to noises serving us as warnings- alarms, sirens, and oven timers. They are also aware of our mechanical world, full of ticking, clicking, and whirring devices. Sounds heard with the cochlear implant can be just as annoying as they are through ears that hear. My children regularly complain about the unbearably loud air conditioner humming next to the tennis courts. Yet, I am thankful they have hearing devices to take in all types of sound. Anything enriching their lives makes the proverbial glass half full. Our senses not only give us practical information but also help us feel the poetry when we live it.

Defining Standards. A thriving Generation CI will eventually require a consistent standard of treatment for learning the skills of listening and speaking. Every child who receives an implant should have access to the best method for acquiring language.

Currently, families across the country are confronted by different approaches to speech therapy with variations in insurance coverage and available programming directing their choices. Learning environments need to be "appropriate" and the "least restrictive" for listening and developing speech and language.

Generation CI will require more consistency across preschool programs as to how these terms are defined. My children have worked within the constructs of a private oral school on the West Coast and a public school IEP on the East Coast, experiencing a wide variety of tactics and philosophies. Private speech schools have to jockey available staff and budget restrictions with physical space limitations, and are naturally influenced by donations more than their public counterparts. Even though our experience in such an environment was overwhelmingly positive during three years of full participation, guidelines for children attending the program were constantly revised according to the above restraints. Our dealings with public programs ranged from totally unacceptable to merely ineffective.

Differences in cochlear implant treatment plans can vary widely. Some speech therapists are able to work every day with a child, while others can only do so once or twice a week. Others may have to work remotely via Skype. I know therapists who see the benefit of having a close relationship with parents, naturally including them as part of the child's team. Yet, other professionals are not as interested in what's going on at home if family counseling is not part of the job description. Variations in available treatments across our country leave many parents at the mercy of chance encounters with local healthcare professionals or place their child in existing and often inadequate state programming.

Do different strategies have alternate outcomes? For my children, the private preschool experience was without a doubt the reason for their success. Should a child be required to have a classroom experience for preschool with teachers trained in oral speech therapy methods who can problem solve cochlear implant malfunctions during the school day? The cochlear implant must be treated like a specific solution to hearing loss, one that has an explicit course of treatment not to be mixed in with other health issues that affect learning. Should state funded programs be run the same as private schools? Consistency across all curricula will strengthen everyone's success, replacing competition with collaboration. Financial issues may prevent certain families from placing their children into private oral schools if scholarships are unavailable. Established national standards should guide the Individual Education Plans (IEPs) of Generation CI, not local resources. It hurts children to have differences across the country, as families are not usually able to relocate for better access to healthcare. My children benefited the most from intense one on one interaction in individual speech therapy sessions and classrooms small enough to allow direct contact between teacher and student.

Worth its weight in gold, the amazing cochlear implant provides a child with the ability to rapidly learn language and speak naturally with intensive speech therapy. Cochlear implant technology keeps up with a child's busy mind, soaking up information effortlessly and accurately. Its general reliability, despite enormous battery consumption and somewhat fragile external parts makes this possible. Generation CI will use cochlear implants to listen without looking and hear without doubting what is heard. A cochlear implant cannot change a child's personality but it will definitely influence who they may become and what gifts they can develop.

During my children's singing lessons, I listen to separate voices blending together until they merge into one pure pitch. Two voices sounding like one. To accomplish this exercise, they must listen to each other and hold the tone simultaneously. If one falters, the dissonance is immediately evident. The note is sung as long as possible, requiring every ounce of air in their lungs. I find this feat and all it requires remarkable.

Of course, not every child of Generation CI will develop at the same rate or to the same extent. As previously discussed, many issues influence the development of a child, including how they learn and process information with new factors being uncovered all the time. Personality will influence if they are outgoing "talkers" or patient "listeners" despite a decent ability to hear. Achieving success with the cochlear implant is based upon a total and complete commitment to the technology, in supporting it and in helping a child make use of it to the best of their ability.

The cost of life circumstances. Children with hearing loss are born into specific life circumstances affecting their progress, including their family's financial means to support and maintain cochlear implants over years of daily use. There are continuing costs to managing cochlear implants and until better standards of care are covered by insurance, families will have to endure a financial commitment to ensure better hearing. Even with the most careful of caretakers, all parts and pieces of my children's cochlear implant equipment have been replaced to some extent at our expense. We have purchased a backup speech processor, microphones and wires so our children will never go without hearing. I buy specialized waterproof bags to keep their speech processors safe from heavy tropical rain and humidity in Florida. Even if they are more expensive, I look for children's shirts loose and opaque enough to keep fanny packs from bulging under clothing.

Unforeseen expenses tied to their cochlear implants continue to mount. My children have their own health insurance to cover basic health costs. Sensorineural profound hearing loss, present at birth is considered a preexisting condition exacerbating the rate of insurance coverage. Audiology appointments are considered the work of a health specialist and we are charged extra fees. Private preschool and therapy sessions for my children were absorbed by the County of San Mateo, California but only after we mediated our arguments in court. It was clear that private speech and language programs were not to be a burden of the State. No matter how complete our children's coverage may be, we have out of pocket costs, such as replacing batteries for traveling emergencies and fanny packs that wear thin after months of rubbing from the momentum of active children.

No one warned us about potential extra expenditures for the cochlear implants or could have predicted their total cost. Regardless, parents with means often devote a substantial portion of income to their children with soccer and piano lessons, private school, the latest Nike tennis shoes and college tuition. For us, the cost of the cochlear implant is part of our parenting responsibilities. Not every family has the resources to adequately support a child's progress. Hearing loss does not discriminate. Hopefully, as Generation CI grows in power and influence, the standard of care will become more affordable for all children. Efficient practices should drive costs down while future legislation aimed at inclusion eliminates denial of coverage.

Key Points to Consider

1. The children of Generation CI will redefine what it means to be born with hearing loss.

2. Be aware of how the cochlear implant heightens your child's experience of the world.

3. Your child's success will influence standards of treatment for all.

20

My Second Year Journal: Rewards of Family

Two years and three months old.

Fifteen months with the implant.

    After fifteen months with the implant, my two-year old child is reaping the rewards of family. Working together we accomplish much. My child is always engaged and interested in the comings and goings of the family. He shows an eagerness to participate in our banter, to be an important part of our activities. This requires listening carefully to all that is happening around him. He initiates a conversation with me by pointing to the sky as an airplane flies overhead. The jet engine's roar draws my gaze upwards. If he cannot see it behind the clouds, he points to his microphone in an effort to tell me, "Can you hear it, Momma? I can!" So many sounds bring joy to a child. What a pleasure to listen together, to hear simultaneously and know we can share the experience. He shadows close behind me when our doorbell chimes, knowing the sound brings his father home from work or a friend over to play. He crawls on my lap anticipating how the telephone draws my attention away from him. From there, he may point to express a desire to watch TV or to a toy high on the shelf. "The Point" is still a powerful way of telling me what words he needs to communicate a thought. His vigorous pointing pays off as I retrieve the puzzle for him to play with at my feet. Spreading the pieces he begins to work, mission accomplished. My child listens and reacts to sounds around him, actively participating in our life at home.

My child voices his place among us when calling family members by name. There are times when only Papa will do, especially when the goal is to go outside and play ball. So, he experiments with intonation, calling "Papa" with urgency to get his father's attention or with joy when he retrieves our soccer ball from the toy box upstairs. Understanding how the tone of his voice communicates, he practices different ways of beckoning me. For reading time together, preparing for meals and to be rocked at night, he shouts "Momma" in frustration or as a question. I sense how my name can be loaded with extra meaning, with a need for help or for comforting after a fall. Best of all, his voice sometimes resonates pure love between mother and child. He yells "Baby!" with rage over his sister's ability to draw my focus away from him or with a sarcastic tone to tease her. Each person in the family is a sounding board to engage and learn from. A name is not just for identification. It represents a personality and a relationship to my child. He has a found a circle of love in which to test his growing knowledge of language and he watches closely how we respond to his voice.

I realize, living abroad, I cannot assume every culture believes in integrating all children into mainstream society. During one of our many evaluations at the Frankfurt hospital, a psychologist tells me, "Even though your child is intelligent, most likely he will not go to university if you stay in Germany. Teachers of mainstream classrooms are not required by law to accept him." An educational system placing youngsters early on a career track does not acknowledge my child's potential *for eventually competing with or surpassing his peers academically. We aim to have our child mainstreamed in a school with hearing children by kindergarten, a goal often achieved when early intervention is successful.*

On our speech therapist's recommendation, my husband and I tour a special school where German children board away from their families to receive speech and language therapy. How sad to see mothers sitting in the school's waiting room for visitations. It seems counterproductive for families to suffer from the separation as well. We could never leave the fate of our children to strangers, preferring to take on the responsibility ourselves. It's not an easy choice for us, but ultimately the most productive one. We know no one will ever advocate for them as we do. Reflecting on the attitudes and social boundaries we encountered, I remain unconvinced they would have had the same opportunities if we had stayed in Europe.

Although we still have far to go, my husband and I conceive an action plan we know can be carried out together to best care for our children. We realize they should be raised in the United States and attend a school specializing in cochlear implants to learn alongside other children like themselves. They must be immersed in American English to acquire language quickly. They will always need an audiologist nearby who can test cochlear implant equipment and a source for buying cables, microphones and battery cases. We will need the school to welcome us as part of the solution with education and support. We made sure the move was in line with our choices for the children and their cochlear implants.

Driving along the Rhine River from Wiesbaden, we head to a farewell lunch with friends at the picturesque Kloster Eberbach, a former German monastery now open to the public. In a few weeks, we will be leaving Europe for the misty shores of the Bay Area in California. After evaluating "Oral Deaf Education" preschools online and speaking with program directors, we decide on a well-established school in Redwood City. There both children will be able to attend preschool, have speech therapy and see the audiologist. Our daughter will have her cochlear implant surgery at the Stanford Hospital in Palo Alto when she is eleven months and her programming will be done at the California Ear Institute. We work to make the transition a smooth one for the family.

For our children's sake, we choose to live in a nation where anyone with hearing loss can be led by their dreams. Only in a country where the basic freedoms and rights of all people are protected-- at least in theory, will they be able to demand equal treatment. We want them to grow up knowing they can pursue any field of study or occupation without discrimination. Our laws are aimed at preventing children with hearing loss from being left behind, safeguarding inclusiveness in mainstream classrooms.

Even when actual policy fails to provide the best environments for children with cochlear implants, the ideology of inclusion remains a strong deep-seated part of our society. Americans can no longer justify mistreating a subgroup of society as a "lesser" one, deserving less privileges and rights. Even when the question of equality in America is still unresolved, our children will grow up in a land where they can demand fair treatment.

Freedom of Speech also empowers advocates of sign language to spread arguments against cochlear implants in periodicals, newspapers and on the Internet. Their passionate criticisms seem to be driven by the fear of losing status as a separate identity, a Deaf culture with a special language of its own. Establishing cochlear implants as the recommended treatment for profound hearing loss will without a doubt abate the necessity of sign language. With proof of its success, the trend towards cochlear implants also puts at risk many of the benefits currently enjoyed by the Deaf.

Somehow, arguments against the cochlear implant always distract from the reality that humans were meant to hear. There must be a reason for it. If I as a parent can give my child better hearing, why would I choose not to? Why would I not want my children to speak my own language if it is possible? Parents of infants with profound hearing loss must understand the real outcomes of their choice either to have their child learn only sign language or learn to listen and speak. It only takes spending the day at an oral deaf school, observing children with cochlear implants listening and speaking for parents to see first hand the potential of the cochlear implant.

Our family has found a rhythm to live by even if we drum to a different beat. With time, the unexpected becomes routine and the unusual morphs into familiarity. My son has been in the hearing world for almost a year and a half. Life for him began without sound and now I hear him call, "Papa", "Momma", and "Baby" with a clear voice. Looking back, I am overwhelmed by the seemingly trivial events recorded in my journal. I now realize my entries were only a few of the countless accomplishments my son has achieved in learning to listen and speak. If I could actually record everything he did, I would fill a library to his credit. Thankfully, it was not necessary to identify each piece of the progress. A system of learning was established and I had proof of it in my journal.

The learning continues. Together, we replace "da-da-da" with new words as situations engage his interest. He watches our mouths closely when he is trying to learn a new word but he is not dependent on visual assistance for the words he already knows. Achieving proficiency in anything requires discipline and patience.

Without hearing loss, children absorb language without trying, like Vitamin D from the sun. I watch parents everywhere, in line at the grocery store or in the waiting room of our pediatrician, constantly teaching new words to their children and correcting errors in speech. The difference for me is how conscious I am of the consequences of letting my son down, of not having batteries or a new microphone to replace the broken one or not listening when he tries to speak. I know the work to learn language begins with me as parent of two children with hearing loss, embedded in my choices how to raise my children and how I fill my time each day.

My determination is boundless. I will do anything for my children, even if it means I will read to them when I am tired at night. I will listen and try to understand even if I am in a hurry. I make a promise to them. Together, we will change their destiny. They, children born without hearing, will learn to listen and speak.

I believe my son's knowledge of vocabulary will eventually equal his peers. I don't see any reason why he won't be able to keep learning the meaning of new words. There is no limit to *his capabilities. My journaling will evolve as his language becomes more sophisticated. I anticipate the need to begin a list of superfluous words, such as "like" and "actually". My child will also need to learn slang to keep up as a teen. Knowing the definition of a word is only the first step.*

My child signals the end of the day with a quick wave and the sounds "a-da" to the melody of "goodbye" or "goodnight". I know what he is trying to say. He is learning to retrieve the best words he can to articulate his thoughts. Then, he evaluates the effect of his word choices on others. I dim the lights and gently rock him while softly singing a song, saying goodnight to each member of our family. "Goodnight Momma, goodnight Momma, goodnight Momma. It's time for you to sleep." Each person in the family is acknowledged by name. Hearing my child say, "Mamma", "Papa" and "Baby", warms my heart. I know he now understands the most beautiful sounds heard through his cochlear implant is the language binding us together. You are my mother and I call you by name.